SCRIPTURE AND THE FAITH

scripture and the faith

BY

a. G. hebert

of the Society of the Sacred Mission

MOREHOUSE-BARLOW COMPANY

New York

First published in the United States
of America in 1962 by arrangement
with Geoffrey Bles · The Centenary Press

CONTENTS

I.	PRESENT PERPLEXITIES	*page* 13
II.	THE FAITH OF ISRAEL—I	23
III.	THE FAITH OF ISRAEL—II	34
IV.	THE NEW TESTAMENT FULFILMENT	45
V.	THE BIBLE AS HISTORY	56
VI.	THE BIBLE TEACHING	67
VII.	THE BIBLE IN THE LITURGY	77
VIII.	THE BIBLE IN THE CHURCH TODAY	87

PREFACE

THERE is something that makes the Bible different from all other books. There are many other religious books, such as the sacred books of Hinduism, or the Jewish Talmuds, or the Mohammedan Koran, or the theological and devotional literature of the Christian Church, but the Bible is not simply one among the sacred books of the world. It claims to speak with authority, as in some special sense the Book of God; and all the other books which we have mentioned, except the Hindu books, appeal to it in some way as authoritative. By the Jewish and the Christian writers the Old Testament is regarded as inspired. The Koran, while treating the Christian Bible with a certain respect, sets itself up as the bible of a rival religion, and endeavors to take its place. Yet the Bible is a human book, and bears on every page the marks of the different outlooks of its human authors.

The Bible is the Book of Israel, and its various writings were all written to bear witness to the Faith of Israel. No better title could be found for the Bible than that of "The Book of the Divine Kingdom", or "The Book of the Faith". The books of the Old Testament were written to tell "the old, old story" of God's choice of Israel to be His people: of His promises to Abraham, of His deliverance of His people from bondage in Egypt, and of His covenant with them at Sinai, whereby they became His people and He their God; of His subsequent dealings with them, of the lessons which they were set to learn about Him and the way of His spiritual service,

5

and of the hopes of a future day in which He would
complete His good purpose for them in the promised
messianic age. The New Testament tells how this purpose of God, begun under the Old Covenant, has been
fulfilled in the coming of Jesus, His ministry and teaching, His death, resurrection and ascension, and the
outpouring of the Spirit at Pentecost. Thereby Israel,
God's chosen people, has been re-constituted as the
Church open to all nations, through which the divine
salvation is to come to the whole world.

The Church, therefore, has had a continuous history,
covering not only the nineteen centuries which have
elapsed since the time of our Lord and His Apostles, but
more like thirty-four centuries in all, since the days when
Israel first began to be a nation in the time of Moses;
and the Bible is the book which gives the authoritative
record of the story of God's dealings with His chosen
people, from the beginning of all down to the point at
which the work of salvation is complete, and Church
history is ready to begin. The Bible tells the story of
God's covenant with Israel, and the consummation of
His purpose in the New Covenant; Church history, of
which some important pages are being written in the
events of our own day, is the story of what has happened
since the nations of the world began to enter on the
promises made to Abraham.

Thus the Bible is the Book of the Faith. No one can
rightly understand the Old Testament unless he reads it
in the light of the Faith which Israel believed: and no
one can rightly understand the Bible as a whole, unless
he sees it in the light of the Creed, which is the summary
of the Faith of Israel as it has been fulfilled in Christ, and
of the sacraments whereby the salvation which God has

provided for mankind is conveyed to the Church of every time and place.

The Old Testament is not out of date. From it, and it alone, we can learn what was the work which Jesus the Messiah came to do; for the New Testament at every point appeals to the Old Testament in order to explain who Jesus is and what He has done. We shall see in Chapter III of this book something of the messianic hope announced by the prophets, and in Chapter IV how the New Testament shows how at each point that hope has been fulfilled. The preparation for Christ in the Old Testament is also the preparation of the people themselves, by their education in those spiritual and moral principles which we see them learning in the course of the Old Testament history; and those lessons are no less necessary for us and for every nation which enters on Israel's inheritance. Therefore we still need the Old Testament scriptures for our instruction in the way of God's service, and we pray and praise God in the words of the psalms.

To us therefore, in the fullest sense, the Bible is the Book of the Faith. We believe that God has revealed Himself and has redeemed mankind by His action in history. Our Lord was crucified under Pontius Pilate, and He rose from death on the third day. Those are events in history, and they are the climax of the long series of events which had begun with Abraham and Moses. The divine work of salvation in both Testaments is summed up in the words used daily in the Church's Morning Prayer: "Blessed be the Lord God of Israel, for he hath visited and redeemed his people."

Because the Faith rests on the divine action in history, it is different in kind from all religions which depend only on the teachings of holy and good men. For that reason, it can claim to be no mere doctrine of a God whom men have made in their own image, but to be the revelation of the true and living God who has made them in His. To the Christian Faith there is no rival today—no other belief exists which can even begin to answer the questions about the world and our life, which we believe God has answered for us through His revelation of Himself through Israel His people and Jesus His Son, the Messiah of Israel. When people fall away from that faith, they do not take up with some rival faith, for none such exists; they drop away into unbelief. The fact that many do so drop away is not due to any defect in the Faith; it is due to the failure of us Christians, in past generations and in this, to grasp the meaning of the Faith and to express it worthily in our worship and in our lives.

We need therefore to go back, again and again, to the Bible, to the Creed and the sacraments, and wait on God, as the old prophets and psalmists waited on Him, believing that He who visited and redeemed His people in His mighty works in the past is still carrying out His purpose of salvation for His world. "Israel" still exists: it is the visible Church.

This little book, then, has been written in order to "give a line" about the understanding of the Bible, in the first place for Christian people who go to Church and are familiar with the Church's services, in which (as we shall see especially in Chapters VII and VIII) the Bible takes the chief place. It deals with a great subject, which naturally presents many difficulties to which no quick and easy answers can be given: above all, there is the problem of the inspiration of the Bible—that is to say, of the way in which God has spoken His word through imperfect human writers. In a book such as this, it is impossible to attempt more than, as I have said, to "give a line"; and the positions which are here taken up are justified at greater length in my larger book, *The Authority of the Old Testament.* I owe an acknowledgement to its publishers, Messrs. Faber & Faber, for their ready willingness that this smaller book should appear, dealing with the same theme. The smaller book, however, is very far from being a mere summary of the other; it is an independent treatment of the subject, and in those places where the two texts run parallel for a few pages, it is usually the smaller book that deals with the point in question in greater detail than the other.

A. G. HEBERT, S.S.M.

St George's Priory
   Kelham,
      Newark.

SCRIPTURE AND THE FAITH

CHAPTER I

PRESENT PERPLEXITIES

I T ought to be disturbing to us to find that our present-day methods in the teaching and understanding of the Faith are at variance with those of the New Testament, but that is the case with regard to the way in which subjects so important as the death and resurrection of our Lord are commonly expounded.

Anyone who goes to hear a sermon about our Lord's passion in one of our churches will, as likely as not, find himself listening to a psychological study of one or other of the actors in the story; it may be St. Peter, or Pilate, or the women of Jerusalem. Their motives will be analysed, their attitude to our Lord described; and the preacher's aim will be to help each individual hearer to examine his own motives and be stirred to a deeper devotion. At Easter one may perhaps hear a similar psychological study of St. Mary Magdalene or St. Thomas, or one may hear a doctrinal exposition of the atonement, or of the resurrection of the body.

The New Testament writers do indeed relate with much detail the events of the Lord's death and resurrection (St. Paul devotes a chapter, I Corinthians 15, to the doctrine of the resurrection of the body), but the striking feature of their handling of these subjects, and the point at which they differ from the modern preacher, is that they are continually referring to the Old Testament, either by quoting it directly, or by alluding to it in their choice of phrases; and it is by use of the Old Testament that they habitually explain the meaning of the events which they are describing. St. Mark, in telling the story of the Crucifixion, shows that

13

he is all the time picturing our Lord as the Sufferer of
Psalm 22 by at least three direct quotations—of the
words "They shake their heads", "They part my gar-
ments among them", and "My God, my God, look upon
me, why hast thou foresaken me?"—in Mark 15:29, 24,
34. St. Peter, in the well-known passage which is read
for the Epistle on the Second Sunday after Easter,
adapts a string of texts from the fifty-third chapter of
Isaiah: "Although he had done no violence, neither was
any deceit in his mouth"; "He was oppressed yet he
humbled himself, and opened not his mouth"; "Surely
he hath borne our griefs and carried our sorrows";
"He bare the sin of many, and made intercession for
the transgressors"; "With his stripes we are healed";
"All we like sheep have gone astray" (Isaiah 53:9, 7, 4,
12, 5, 6). I Peter 2:22-25 consists almost wholly of a
free quotation of these texts. As for the Resurrection,
explicit allusion is made to the Exodus from Egypt and
the Covenant at Sinai in the account of Moses and
Elijah speaking with our Lord at His transfiguration of
His "decease" (but the Greek word is *exodos*) which
He should accomplish at Jerusalem (Luke 9:31); in
St. Paul's "Christ our passover is sacrificed for us"
(I Corinthians 5:7); in St. John's description of Him
as the Lamb of God (John 1:29)—that is, God's paschal
lamb, of which it was written, "A bone of it shall be not be
broken" (John 19:36, quoting Exodus 12:46)—and in
His own words at the Last Supper, "This is my blood
of the covenant" (Mark 14:24, alluding to Exodus
24:8).

The liturgical tradition of the Church is here in line
with that of the apostolic writers, and at variance with
our usual habit today. On Good Friday we recite Psalm

22; at Easter, Psalm 114, "When Israel came out of Egypt." We sing in our Easter hymns how God has

> Loosed from Pharaoh's bitter yoke,
> Jacob's sons and daughters;
> Led them with unmoistened foot
> Through the Red Sea waters.
> *(Hymn 94)*

and the same manner of describing our Lord's redeeming work in terms of the deliverance of Israel from Egypt occurs again and again in the ancient form for the blessing of the paschal candle, which is used in very many of our churches on Easter Eve. Instances could be multiplied almost without limit. At all the great festivals we have a similar use of the Old Testament; at Christmas we hear for the first lesson Isaiah's prophecies of the birth of the Messiah and of His reign, and at Epiphany the prophecies of the manifestation of God's glory to the Gentile world, in order that we may put the Old Testament texts side by side with their Christian fulfilment, and thereby be helped to enter into the meaning of the Saviour's birth and the work that He came on earth to do. It is the same with the Psalms. On Ascension Day, Christ is the King of Glory, at whose coming the heavenly gates lift up their heads (Psalm 24:7), as He is the man who "leadeth an uncorrupt life, and doeth the thing which is right, and speaketh the truth from his heart", who alone is worthy to "dwell in God's tabernacle, and rest upon his holy hill" (Psalm 15:1-2, cf. 24:3-4). On Whitsunday, when the Holy Ghost descends upon the Church, we have at Evening Prayer, Psalm 48, "Great is the Lord, and highly to be praised: in the city of our God, even upon his holy

hill", and Psalm 68, "Let God arise and let his enemies
be scattered"—a quotation of the anthem that was sung
when the sacred Ark went out to battle (see Numbers
10:35).

Yet it is relatively rare, in most churches, for the use
of the Old Testament in the New Testament and in the
liturgy to be explained from the pulpit; indeed, there is
widespread perplexity about the Old Testament among
both clergy and laity. People have a sense that they have
somehow fallen out of sympathy with it, and do not know
what to make of it. Since this is for the most part a vague
feeling of uncertainty which does not find any precise or
clear expression, it is not easy to define it exactly; and it
seems, indeed, to take several rather different forms,
springing from different causes.

Sometimes it seems to spring out of a reaction against
the old-fashioned Protestant bibliolatry, which treated
the Old Testament as if it stood on a level with the New,
and seemed to end in being a religion of Scripture texts
and to stop short of the mystery of our Lord's cradle,
and of His cross, and of His living sacramental presence.
The vital thing seemed to be to return to a living religion
centered round the altar, and gain an intense realization
of our Lord's presence in His Church as our living Saviour. Many who stood outside the Catholic movement
in the Church have never understood that it was an
ardent desire to seek "Jesus only" which produced a crop
of what seemed to them strange ritualistic rites, and a
seeming coldness towards the Old Testament. It is easy
to say now that movements of reaction involve exagger-
ation; yet it is true that the Old Testament is pre-Christian, is in itself imperfect, and needs to be fulfilled in the
New.

The fact that the Old Testament is pre-Christian, lies at the root of the difficulties felt by very many Christian people. They are aware of the criticisms of the Bible made by those who are veiled or open enemies of the Faith; they do not see how to answer such objections, and indeed are themselves troubled by them. They know that it is constantly said that the creation-story in the Book of Genesis is at variance with the truth as science has discovered it: Adam and Eve never existed: and how could a flood which covered the earth to a depth of twenty-five feet (Genesis 7:20) have deposited the ark on Mount Ararat? There are many narratives whose historical truth is known to be called in question. Then there are the moral difficulties: why is Saul said to have been commanded by the Lord to exterminate the Amale-kites, and why do the "cursing psalms" invoke ven-geance on enemies, in a way that seems quite contrary to the spirit of our Lord, who commanded us to love our enemies, and Himself prayed for His murderers?

They have further difficulties about the use of the Old Testament. It seems hard to see the relevance to our daily life of many of the lessons read in church; there often appears to be little that is edifying in the stories of Israel's wanderings in the wilderness, or of the reigns of Jehu or Uzziah. That is indeed no new problem; Origen in the third century tells how the people were troubled by it then, and he could solve it only by wholesale allegorical interpretations. Then again, the prophets are hard to understand, and so, often, are the psalms; would it not be better to sing Christian hymns instead? What is one to make of "Moab is my wash-pot, over Edom will I cast out my shoe: Philistia, be thou glad of me" (Psalms 60:8 and 108:9)? A gleam of light may seem to come in the next verse: "Who will lead me into the strong city: and who will bring me into Edom?' which may suggest the thought of the victory of Christ over the powers of evil and the establishment of His Kingdom, but the general problem remains. It comes to this: Why should Christians be thus expected to express their prayer and praise in the Semitic manner, and be continually identifying the successes and failures of the ancient Jews with their own?

By those who stand more or less outside the Church such things are levelled as reproaches against us. In our day it is becoming increasingly common to find a real hostility against the Bible, resting on a more or less avowed antagonism to the Christian faith. One is never surprised to meet a sneer against the Old Testament in a newspaper article, or a speech, or a school lesson. Perhaps it is a jibe against the bloodthirsty morality of some Bible story, perhaps against the fabulous element in it. There is met the continual assumption, resting on a materialistic attitude of mind, that the only truth that matters is the matter-of-fact truth of natural science or of history: that which is true is that which is capable of being verified by the senses, or by historical proof. The account of the Creation cannot be true if it does not square with the facts established by modern astronomy, geology and biology. The Old Testament is judged from a purely historical point of view, and the story is taken to be simply that of the emergence of a pugnacious Semitic tribe from a state of primitive savagery (represented, for instance, by the story of Jael the wife of Heber the Kenite) to an admittedly high level of religion and morals. If that be so, the earlier parts of the Old Testament can have little value for us.

Many of the answers given by Christian teachers to such questions do not satisfactorily meet the case. The materialistic attitude of mind is indeed countered by the affirmation that there is such a thing as religious truth, a truth about the things not seen, to which also the poet, the painter, and the musician bear witness; but the moral difficulty about the Bible is often met by the assertion that there are in it "degrees of inspiration", ranging from the low level of some of the early narratives and the unedifying genealogies and laws, to the high inspiration of the great prophets and psalmists. Those were true men of God; their writings reflect a deep and noble religious experience; and the Church in every age needs to read and ponder on the wonderful vision of God's glory in Isaiah, Chapter 6, the poems of the "Servant of the Lord" which come later on in Isaiah, and the psalms which speak of God's glory in the created world, such as Psalm 19, "The heavens declare the glory of God", or His care for His people, as Psalm 23, "The Lord is my shepherd".

It is true, and important, that those prophets and psalmists were men of God; it is also true, beyond doubt, that they show depths of wisdom and insight which some of the other writers do not share (it is so in the New Testament also; not every New Testament writer is a St. John), but it is unsatisfactory to cut up the Bible, in this way to attempt to separate those parts which we ourselves find specially edifying and inspiring, and relegate to a lower level those which seem to us inferior. When that is done, it becomes no longer possible to regard the Bible as a whole as God's book; the logical conclusion is that we should substitute for it a Biblical anthology, consisting of a selection of the "best" passages.

That will not do. It is not possible rightly to understand even the parts that we like best by isolating them from the whole to which they belong; and it is the Old Testament as a whole that has been accepted as inspired and as the word of God by our Lord and His Apostles and the Church. The problem of the Bible cannot be solved by cutting it up into little pieces. Very many today are aware of the urgent need to find a way to see the Bible as a whole to be God's book, without wishing that certain parts of it were not there. Whatever may be its real (as contrasted to its alleged) imperfections, God had a meaning in them all. It is the Bible as a whole that tells the story of His dealings with His people Israel.

It will be our aim in this book to give some help in this direction: to show how the Bible is the Book of the Faith, to try to take a positive and constructive view of the Old Testament, and to see the relation in which it stands to the New Testament, and so gain a view of the unity of the Bible, and learn what the Church means by the use which it makes of it in its liturgy.

It is necessary to begin with the literal meaning of the Old Testament. We cannot solve our problems by trying to put the clock back, and simply return to the patristic or medieval view; for our modern interest in the matter-of-fact truth of history is right enough in itself, and it is a gift of God to our age. It is the same with the critical study of the Bible as it is with modern discoveries in the field of natural science and the labor-saving inventions to which they have given rise. Just as we need to thank God for our electric light, our automobiles and television, and recognize that the misuse of those things which makes our modern world unhappy and restless is due to the sin of man and his failure to co-ordinate his natural activities with his spiritual nature and his divine calling; so we ought to be able to accept gladly all the fuller knowledge which modern scholarship and discovery has brought to us in regard to the Bible, while at the same time keeping hold of the Christian understanding of it as God's inspired book, which the tradition of the Church has handed down.

Recent scholarship is indeed giving much help in precisely that direction. It is now being more clearly seen that, as the books of the New Testament were all written within the Church to testify to the faith in the Lord's resurrection on which the Church is founded, so the Old Testament books were written within Israel—that is, within the same Church at the pre-Christian stage of its existence—to testify to the faith of Israel in the living God who had chosen Israel to be His people. The formation of those books into a Canon of Scripture took place largely through the liturgical use of them in the synagogue. Synagogues began to exist, as we shall see later on in this book, during the exile; there is no record of their actual beginning, but they certainly became an important factor in the life of Israel after the exile, as they were in our Lord's day. In them was evolved that four-fold pattern of service, consisting of prayer and praise and the reading and expounding of the Scriptures which we still use today, as for instance in the ordinary Sunday Morning or Evening Prayer. Side by side with the synagogue in ancient Judaism stood the Temple with its sacrifices. In the Church, the first part of the traditional eucharistic liturgy has come down by direct descent from the synagogue service, while the latter part, beginning with the Offertory, consists of the sacrificial rite which our Lord instituted in the night that He was betrayed.

We shall have to see, further, how the New Testament writers use the Old Testament, and how their use of it is continued in the Christian liturgical tradition. We have already had a glimpse of that at the beginning of this chapter; later on we must see in more detail how the Apostles in the New Testament show the Old Testament to be completed and fulfilled in the Christian Gospel. "Think not that I came to destroy the law or the prophets", He Himself said; "I am not come to destroy, but to fulfill" (Matthew 5:17). If we can gain a clear view of the meaning of the New Testament's use of the Old, we shall have gained a conception of the unity of the Bible as a whole: of a divine purpose of salvation begun in the story of the one nation of Israel, and made complete in the work of Christ, His death and resurrection and the coming of the Holy Ghost, and continuing in the Church which is the New Israel, open to people of all nations. Such a conception involves necessarily a "spiritual" or "mystical" interpretation of the Old Testament. It is necessary, as the best theologians have always asserted, to begin with the plain and literal meaning of it; but a further spiritual interpretation is plainly present in our Lord's own use of it, as well as in that of His Apostles. Thus it is necessary to find a way to distinguish the right and justifiable spiritual interpretation from that sort of allegorical interpretation which is arbitrary and fanciful.

We shall then be concerned in the first place with the interpretation of the Bible in the common worship of the Church, rather than with its private devotional use. In its liturgy the Church sees the Bible as one whole, and teaches us so to use it; our private use of it for meditation and devotion is dependent on the public use of it in Church services. The liturgical use of the Bible, which

is provided in the Book of Common Prayer on the same
lines as in the older rites of Christendom, is the best of
all schools for the right understanding of the Bible.
When its lessons are truly learned, there can be nothing
but gain in the fuller light which is thrown on the original
and literal meaning by the methods of modern scholarship.

We will begin, then, in the next chapter, with the con-
sideration of the literal meaning of the Old Testament as
it stands, approaching it as the Book of Israel's Faith.

CHAPTER II

The Faith of Israel—I

T HE Bible has a preface (Genesis 1-11), and an introduction (Genesis 12-end), before its main theme
develops. We shall see, in this chapter and the next, how
its main theme can be summarized in three statements of
faith, representing the middle period of the monarchy,
the period of the exile, and the apostolic age respectively;
for the main theme is the story of Israel, God's chosen
people, and of His saving purpose, which reaches its
consummation in the story of Jesus, the Messiah of
Israel and the Saviour of the world. The Bible, therefore,
ends with the Apostle's witness to Jesus, and with the
preaching of the divine salvation to all nations; in the
last book of the Bible we read the song of praise to Jesus
the Christ, sung by the four living creatures and the

four-and-twenty elders: "Worthy art thou to take the book and to open the seals thereof; for thou wast slain, and didst purchase to God with thy blood men of every tribe and tongue and people and nation, and madest them to be unto our God a kingdom and priests, and they reign upon the earth" (Revelation 5:9-10).

Fittingly, then, the preface to the Bible begins not with the beginning of the story of Israel, but with the beginning of the universe and of man. "In the beginning God created the heaven and the earth." "And God created man in his own image: in the image of God created he him: male and female created he them." "And God saw everything that he had made, and behold, it was very good" (Genesis 1:1, 27, 31).

The second story of Genesis (Chapter 2, beginning at verse 4) tells of the place of man in the created world. The key to its right understanding is that "Adam" is not a proper name, but is simply the Hebrew word for "Man". The story is told by the writer in the language of myth, which is the proper and necessary vehicle for the expression of the truth which he has to convey. The place of man in relation to the earth is given in the words: "The Lord God took the man, and put him into the garden of Eden, to dress it and to keep it" (verse 15)— to till the ground and cultivate it, to make himself a home, to build up a civilization. He is free to do what he will, subject to a prohibition which expresses the fact that he belongs to God and is under God's law; of every tree in the Garden he may freely eat, except for one tree of which he may not eat (verses 16-17). He is surrounded by the animals, and he gives them names; but they cannot provide "a help meet for him" and satisfy his need for social fellowship (verses 18-20). That he is given in Eve his wife ("Eve" is the Hebrew for "life", or "life-giving"—Genesis 3:20); and when he sees her, he bursts into the primal song of Man's love for Woman: *"This* is now bone of my bones and flesh of my flesh: *this* shall be called Woman: for *this* was taken out of Man" (Chapter 2, verse 23, from the Hebrew).

Such is the true place of man in relation to the earth, to the animals and to his wife, according to God's law for man; but such is not man's actual condition as we know it. The story continues: The Man and the Woman chose to transgress the order which God had established for them, because they wanted to be "as God, knowing good and evil". "To know good and evil" in the Bible does not mean to know the distinction between right and wrong, but to know what is advantageous and what is harmful, to have sagacity or prudence, to possess discretion. God intended such knowledge for them anyhow, for He had made them capable of it; but they chose to grasp at it greedily and have it for themselves in their own way, disobeying His prohibition; they chose to develop and build up their civilization without regard to God and His ordinance (Chapter 3:1-6). After the fatal step has been taken, we notice not only that they are afraid of God (verse 8), but also that the Man has forgotten his old loving reverence for his wife; she is now to him "the woman whom thou gavest to be with me" (verse 12); he thinks of her no longer as bone of his bones and flesh of his flesh, but as another individual with whom he must live as best as he can. Also the ground is "cursed for man's sake" (verse 17); his work has become drudgery. Soon we read that "all flesh has corrupted its way upon the earth" (Genesis 6:12); then comes the story of the Flood, the type of all God's

judgments on sinful man, with the ark as the type of
God's salvation for man out of the midst of His
judgments.

Such is the preface to the Bible. The world is good; it
is God's world, and man's life is set in the midst of God's
created order. The way of life for man is to live subject
to the God to whom he belongs; the way of death for
man is to love the self in place of God: it is said to man
that when he transgresses that order "thou shalt surely
die" (Genesis 2:17). That man has chosen the way of
death is the sorrowful fact; to see that all flesh has corrupted its way upon the earth we have only to read the
morning paper, or to look into our own hearts. This
view of the actual state of the world, that it is a dark and
sinful world, is the presupposition of the whole Bible, and
the background of the whole story that follows, both in
the Old Testament and in the New.

That being so, what has God done about it? The Bible
goes on to tell the story of man's salvation. That salvation reaches its final expression in the words: "God so
loved the world, that he gave his only-begotten Son, that
whosoever believeth in him should not perish, but have
everlasting life" (John 3:16), but much had to happen
before the time was come for that. God had to take Himself a nation, make it His chosen people, educate it in the
way of His spiritual service and purify it through suffering, before He could provide the final remedy for sin
through the sacrifice of His Son. That is the main story,
but before it begins, we have the Introduction.

The introduction begins with the call of Abraham.
"Now the Lord said unto Abraham, Get thee out of thy
country and from thy kindred and from thy father's
house, unto the land that I will show thee; and I will

make thee a great nation, and I will bless thee, and make thy name great . . . and in thee shall all the families of the earth be blessed" (Genesis 12:1-3). Abraham is the man of faith, who receives God's promises, and is prepared to make the venture of faith in obedience to His will. Henceforth in the midst of the dark and sinful world there is to be a nucleus of people who believe in God, call upon His Name, and look to the consummation of His purpose of salvation. Abraham receives God's blessing; and it is Abraham's blessing that is inherited by Isaac (Genesis 26:2-6), of whom we are told little, and by Jacob (Genesis 35:11-12), of whom we are told much because he is the father of the fathers of the Twelve Tribes of Israel. His story and that of Joseph bring us to the threshold of the main story.

The main story begins at the book of Exodus, with the redemption of Israel from bondage in Egypt, the crossing of the Red Sea, and the making of the Covenant of God with Israel at Sinai or Horeb, whereby Israel becomes the people of God. The mighty acts of God in delivering Israel out of Egypt are constantly referred to by prophets and psalmists as the crucial divine acts by which Israel was constituted as God's chosen people. As Christian devotion always goes back to the crucial events of the second Redemption—to the birth at Bethlehem, the death on the cross, the resurrection on the third day, the ascension, the outpouring of the Spirit—and as Christian worship therefore centers round the Memorial of His sacrificial death which He instituted on the night of His passion, so the faith of Old Israel always went back to the events of the first Redemption:

"When Israel was a child, then I loved him, and called my son out of Egypt" (Hosea 11:1).

"When Israel came out of Egypt, and the house of
Jacob from among the strange people,
Judah was his sanctuary, and Israel his dominion"
(Psalm 114:1-2).

"When thy son asketh thee in time to come, What
mean the testimonies, and the statutes, and the judgments, which the Lord our God hath commanded you?
then shalt thou say unto thy son, We were Pharoah's
bondmen in Egypt; and the Lord showed signs and
wonders, great and sore, upon Egypt, and upon Phar-
aoh, and upon all his house, before our eyes; and he
brought us out from thence, that he might bring us
into the land which he sware unto our fathers".
(Deuteronomy 6:20-23).

The first Redemption, like the second, is a divine work
of deliverance wrought in history. If either the one or the
other were myth and not history, the basis of our faith
would be destroyed; yet the very fact that the story of
the Exodus was the basis of Israel's faith, and therefore
was handed down from father to son and told and re-
told afresh in every generation—just as we are continually retelling and re-expressing in sacred art and song
the "old, old story" of our salvation through Christ—
makes it difficult for us now to get a clear picture of the
actual events; for in the Book of the Exodus several
versions of the story have been woven in with one another, so that the narrative of the plagues, for instance, is
somewhat cumbrous and overloaded. Scholars, however,
are able to distinguish the different strands, and then
we see how each narrative taken separately moved by a
swift and dramatic succession of events to the tremendous climax, when Israel, caught in a seemingly hopeless
position between the sea and the fortified frontier be-

tween Suez and the Mediterranean to the east, and the
pursuing Egyptian army to the west, found in the dead
of night that the sea had receded before them, and hur-
ried across; and then, as dawn broke, the Egyptians
following them were overwhelmed, probably by a mighty
tidal wave following a volcanic eruption lower down in
the Red Sea. The unforgettable memory is expressed in
the ancient poem in Exodus 15:21—

"Sing ye to the Lord, for he hath triumphed gloriously;
The horse and his rider hath he thrown into the sea".

The earliest written narrative is believed to have been
written about the time of Elijah; and if we had asked a
faithful Israelite of that date (about 850 B.C.) to draw
up a statement of his faith, he would have expressed it
somewhat thus: "The Lord our God delivered us out of
Egypt with a mighty hand and an outstretched arm; He
made His Covenant with us at Horeb, that we might be
His people and He be our God; He brought us into the
promised land of Canaan, where now we dwell; and now
we hope that we shall live in peace under His protection,
that He may fufill His good purpose with us." That is
the first of our three statements of faith.

Israel was then in Canaan. David had conquered Jerusalem, and Solomon had built the Temple; the nation had
become divided into two kingdoms, but it retained the
consciousness of being one people. During that whole
period a conflict was going on between the ancient faith
of Israel in the Lord God, and the nature-religions of the
Canaanites. Israel in the wilderness had been a nomadic
people, with flocks and herds; but when they settled in
Canaan and became an agricultural people, they learned
the arts of agriculture from their Canaanite neighbors;
and that meant, in turn, that they learned an agricul-

tural religion with a cycle of festivals concerned with the crops and the harvest. There was grave danger, therefore, lest they should lose their ancient faith, forsake the Lord their God, and go after the Canaanite Baals. The Book of Judges represents the conflict as a kind of seesaw between the two; in times of prosperity they lapsed into pagan ways, till there came an invasion of some tribe or other from the desert, and then a "judge" arose, like Gideon (whose story is told in Judges 6-8), who rallied them in the Name of the Lord to repel the enemy, and there was a revival of the national faith. In one form or another the conflict between the religion of the Baals and Israel's faith in the Lord God runs through the whole period of the Judges and the Kings. In the days of Elijah a new danger appeared: the licentious worship of the Tyrian Baal introduced by Jezebel, Ahab's foreign wife.

From that time onwards, while wealth and prosperity were increasing, the political horizon darkened; the national independence was then being threatened by the militaristic empire of Assyria. That was the occasion which raised up the great prophets, Amos and Hosea in the northern kingdom, and Isaiah and Micah in the southern, to warn the people of the danger in which they stood, and accuse them of sin. Amos (who lived about 760 B.C.) is a prophet who is particularly lucid and easy to read. With tremendous power he sought to recall Israel to its faith, denouncing the sins first of a false, unreal, nationalistic religion, a worship without fear of God or repentance for sin (see Amos 3:2; 4:4-5, 12-13; 5:21-24); and then of the oppression of the poor by the rich, the eviction of small farmers from their land, sharp practices in trade, injustice at the courts of law (see Amos 4:1; 5:11-12; 8:4-5). A few years later, Hosea

(who is much more difficult to read) denounced especially the worship of the Canaanite Baals; from his own
grief over the unchastity of Gomer his wife, he learned
how the love of the Lord God for Israel His Bride had
been outraged by the nation which had forsaken Him and
gone after other gods (see Hosea 1:2-3; 2:2-8, 14-17).
In 722 B.C. the threatened judgment came to pass; the
King of Assyria besieged Samaria and took it, and deported the inhabitants to Mesopotamia, and the northern
kingdom came to an end (2 Kings 17:5-23).

The turn of the southern kingdom, Judah, came next.
There was a prolonged "war of nerves", during which the
great Isaiah, prophet, poet, and statesman, stood before
the king and people as a man of unflinching and unshaken
faith in the Lord, while people round him were turning
to any and every religious practice in the hope that if
one sort of sacrifices was in vain, another might avail
(Isaiah 2:6-22; 28:7-16). Meanwhile, politicians turned
to any and every political expedient, such as an alliance
with Egypt, as a gamble which might succeed (Isaiah
30:1-18). Isaiah's faith in the Holy One of Israel was
vindicated when in 701 B.C. Sennacherib's invasion
threatened them with the final disaster, and Isaiah said
that they would be delivered; and so they were (2 Kings
18:13 through Chapter 19; Isaiah 31).

Isaiah had the support of the God-fearing King Heze-
kiah; but the next reign, that of Manasseh, saw a pagan
reaction, and a persecution of the faithful remnant of
Isaiah's disciples (2 Kings 21:1-9, 16). For fifty years
it seemed that all his work had been in vain, but his in-
fluence had gone deep, and in the reign of King Josiah
there came a dramatic change.

In 622 B.C. Hilkiah the high-priest found in the Temple

a "book of the law" (2 Kings 22:8), which probably consisted of the central part of our Book of Deuteronomy, and carried its provisions into effect. There was a wholesale purge of the paraphernalia of the old Canaanite religion and of the new superstitions which had come in more recently; the idol-shrines were destroyed, and all Israel's worship was centralized in the one Temple at Jerusalem (2 Kings 23:4-15; cf. Deuteronomy 12:1-7). There was made a great national confession of faith in the Lord God, and king and people entered into a solemn covenant to serve the Lord God. "The king stood by the pillar, and made a covenant before the Lord, to walk after the Lord, and to keep his commandments and his testimonies and his statutes, with all his heart and with all his soul, to confirm the words of the covenant that were written in this book; and all the people stood to the covenant" (2 Kings 23:3).

It was an occasion of supreme importance in the history of the Faith. It marked the final victory of the faith of Israel in the Lord God over the nature-religions of Canaan. All that was good in the old agricultural religion of the Baals had been incorporated in the worship of the Lord God. The harvest-festival was then kept to His glory; and faith in Him was acknowledged as the regulating principle of the whole national life (see for instance Deuteronomy 15:1-11; 16:13-17, 18-20). The teaching of the prophets was then embodied in a code of laws; but Deuteronomy was not only a law-book; it expressed in glowing exhortations Israel's faith in the Lord who had delivered their forefathers out of Egypt; it proclaimed that He alone was God: "Hear, O Israel; the Lord our God is one Lord: and thou shalt love the Lord God with all thy heart and with all thy soul, and with all thy might. And these words which I command thee this day, shall be upon thy heart; and thou shalt teach them diligently unto thy children, and shalt talk of them when thou sittest in thine house, and when thou walkest by the way, and when thou liest down, and when thou risest up" (Deuteronomy 6:4-7).

It was indeed a great occasion. The Passover was celebrated with much joy; never had there been such a Passover before (2 Kings 23:22). A victory of the Faith had been won, whose results were never undone; yet the immediate sequel was disappointing—times of spiritual joy are often followed by a reaction. King Josiah fell by an untimely death at the age of 39 (2 Kings 23:29); in the people as a whole the devil had been scotched, not killed, and the prophet Jeremiah was faced with a long and discouraging conflict with faithlessness and unbelief through a ministry of forty years. Under a succession of incompetent kings the political situation deteriorated; and when the King of Babylon had defeated first Assyria and then Egypt, he showed himself determined to destroy Judah's national independence. In 597 B.C. he deported 10,000 of the inhabitants of Jerusalem, including the skilled craftsmen and the best of the people (2 Kings 24:10-17); and in 586 B.C. the final blow fell. After a terrible siege of three years, the city was taken, the walls broken down, the temple burnt with fire, and the survivors taken away into exile (2 Kings 24:20; 25:22).

It was the crowning disaster. The national life lay in ruins; its structure was destroyed. It seemed to be the end of everything. There remained only one hope in the completeness of the disaster: it had all been prophesied. Prophet after prophet for a hundred and fifty years, down to the great Jeremiah, had seen it coming, and had said that the Lord God Himself was judging His people for their sins.

CHAPTER III

THE FAITH OF ISRAEL—II

THE Fall of Jerusalem is the central point of the Old Testament history. The national life was then destroyed; Israel died; but because it was the Israel of God, it passed through death to a resurrection. It suffered all that a nation could suffer; but through suffering God taught it the secret of a faith which no amount of suffering could break. The mystery of life arising out of death, which dominates the New Testament, begins to appear already in the Old.

The two prophets who saw Israel through the crisis were Jeremiah and Ezekiel. Ezekiel was among those deported to Babylon in 597 B.C. (Ezekiel 1:1-3); Jeremiah was in Jerusalem through the siege (Jeremiah 27-40). Between the two deportations there were in both places optimists and wishful thinkers who said: It is going to be all right; within a year or two the exiles are going to return, and all will be well (Jeremiah 28:1-4; Ezekiel 13:1-16). Both prophets had to combat those false hopes, and tell the people to expect the worst; and it was the worst that happened (Ezekiel 33:21-22, 30-33).

When it had happened, the mood of the exiles was to say, "Our bones are dried up, our hope is lost; we are clean cut off" (Ezekiel 37:11); why not make the best of it, try to live somehow, and secure a measure of temporal prosperity? Ezekiel observed, in the case of many of his countrymen, that "their heart goeth after their gain" (Chapter 33, verse 31) ; but he continued, whether they would listen or whether they would not, to hammer home relentlessly the lessons, "You have sinned" (*e.g.* Chapter 20). The cogency of the appeal could not be denied, and it was no new message; for 200 years the prophets had been accusing Israel of sin, and announcing God's judgment. Hence it was not open to them to think that Jerusalem had fallen because the Lord had been unable to save His people from disaster. That would have been the case if the God of Israel had been a god like Chemosh of Moab, who was a national figurehead, a personification of the genius of the tribe, like the Britannia on British pennies, or "Miss Liberty" on U.S. silver dollars. On the contrary, the Lord was Himself judging and punishing His people; therefore He was able to save them out of their ruin.

Here is the starting-point of the resurrection of the Faith of Israel in the exile: it is penitence for their sin. Thenceforth Israel became the penitent nation. So it is still; expressions of penitence are a permanent feature of Christian prayer. Out of Israel's penitence, in the exile, sprang the messianic hope; the people were then in a condition to hear the promises of a future divine work of salvation, and the pattern of it emerges clearly in the prophets of the exile.

We are now ready to formulate the second of our three confessions of faith, as it might have been expressed by a disciple of the prophets during the exile. He would say : "Yes, it was all true : the Lord God redeemed us out of Egypt long ago, and made His Covenant with us, and brought us into the promised land; but we sinned fearfully against Him, and He has inflicted on us a fearful

punishment. Now His prophets announce to us that
there is to be a second Exodus: He will redeem us, not
out of Egypt, this time, but from all the countries into
which He has driven us (Jeremiah 23:7-8); He will
make with us a New Covenant, written in our hearts, so
that we shall all know Him, from the least to the greatest of us, and receive the forgiveness of our sin, and be
truly His people, and He our God (Jeremiah 31:31-34);
for He will take away the stony heart out of our flesh,
and give us a heart of flesh, and put His Spirit within us,
that we may keep His commandments and do them
(Ezekiel 36:24-31); He will bring us back to the promised land, and again dwell in our midst, as once His
Presence dwelt on the sacred Ark (Ezekiel 43:1-7;
Isaiah 40:1-11). When that day comes, all nations shall
come to the knowledge of Him, that they may know Him
as we know Him (Isaiah 45:22-25)."

Such was the hope of salvation as it took shape among
the exiles in Babylon in the fifty years after the fall of
Jerusalem. Another great prophet arose, the Second
Isaiah, the author of Isaiah 40-55; through his splendid
preaching Israel became fully conscious of the greatness
of its spiritual inheritance. The people then felt no sense
of inferiority when they watched the imposing religious
processions in honor of the Babylonian gods Bel and
Nebo; those gods were no gods, powerless to do good or
evil (Isaiah 41: 21-29), and the prophet holds up the
idols to contemptuous ridicule (Isaiah 44:8-20). It was
probably at that time that the first chapter of Genesis
was written. It used the language of the creation-myths
of Babylon; but it put into the mouths of the people of
God a story of the creation of the world which would
make the Babylonian myths look foolish.

Second Isaiah's teaching went deeper still. In his prophecy are four poems describing the Servant of the Lord. The Lord's Servant will be humble and patient, devoted to the Lord's service, and will proclaim His Name to the Gentiles (Chapter 42:1-4). In the second poem, the Servant is seen as an instrument in the Lord's hand, like a polished arrow in His quiver; and though discouraged by apparent lack of success, he will effectually become "a light to the Gentiles", to be the means of God's Salvation to the ends of the earth (Chapter 49:1-6). In the third, he is shown as a true disciple, listening morning by morning for the Lord's voice, and patient in enduring personal suffering and persecution (Chapter 50:4-9). The fourth poem (Chapter 52:13 through Chapter 53) consists of five stanzas. (1) It is announced that the Lord's Servant (whom we know from the other poems) "shall deal wisely", or rather "shall prosper": though he suffers, his suffering will lead to exaltation and victory, in a way hitherto undreamt of (Chapter 52:13-15). (2) The people looking on say, "Who hath believed our report?": who (among us) has believed, or understood what we heard? We despised the Servant when we saw him suffer, "we esteemed him not"; we failed to understand (Chapter 53:1-3). (3) They continue: "Surely he hath borne our griefs and carried our sorrows"; now we see that it was for our sin that he was suffering; "with his stripes we are healed" (verses 4-6). (4) Now the prophet speaks, describing the Servant's sufferings, "he was led as a lamb to the slaughter", and was done to death, though there was no deceit in his mouth (verses 7-9); (5) but "it pleased the Lord to bruise him; he hath put him to grief". The martyrdom of the Servant was part of the Lord's own redemptive purpose; and so his soul becomes an offering for sin, an accepted sacrifice, and he who has been numbered with the transgressors and who bare the sin of many, "shall see of the travail of his soul, and shall be satisfied" (verses 10-12).

Every scholar who comments on this passage has to try to answer the question posed with regard to it in Acts 8:34, "Of whom speaketh the prophet this?" It is clear that he is not merely describing the sufferings of the nation; rather he discerns the pattern of the ideal Israelite, of One who should come, in whom God's redemptive purpose should be accomplished. As for the place of his suffering in God's purpose, the prophet has learned that God's people are not merely to look forward in hope to a future time when suffering should be ended, but that somehow their suffering is the means which God has used and will use for His work of salvation itself.

Thus Israel learned the secret of a faith that was stronger than suffering and victorious over death; and Isaiah 53 does not stand alone. Psalm 22, perhaps written about the same time, is the expression in psalm-form of the Servant's prayer. "My God, my God, look upon me, why hast thou forsaken me?" he cries out of a trouble that becomes more and more desperate, till in the middle of verse 21 there is a dramatic change: "from the horns of the wild-oxen—thou hast answered me", and the Psalm ends in a song of victory, glorious and complete, in which all mankind is to share. In Psalm 102 the psalmist begins with expressions of deep grief (verses 1-11); it is the voice of Israel in exile. In verses 12-22 he passes to a strong hope that the Lord will again build up Zion, and will reveal His glory to the Gentiles; and the sign that it is a true hope is that He has put it into the heart of His people to "think upon her stones; and it pitieth them to see her in the dust". He ends with the thought that, though mortal life is short and he himself may not live to see it, yet God's purpose will go forward (verses 23-28).

During the period of the exile the synagogues began (cf. page 21 above). The Israelites, who in the old days had met for worship in the Temple, had in Babylon no place where they could meet; yet during the exile they became a close-knit, believing, and worshipping community. We hear of the elders of Israel meeting in Ezekiel's house (*e.g.* Ezekiel 20:1). At some time or other they began to build houses in which to meet for the reading of the Law and their other sacred writings, and for the training up of the people in a disciplined life of prayer. Many of the psalms are acrostic psalms, each verse beginning with the letters of the alphabet in order (*e.g.* Psalm 25); that was devised as a help to learning them by heart. (Psalm 119, in which the Hebrew letters are still printed in our Bibles, is an acrostic psalm in which each line of each stanza of 8 verses begins with the appropriate letter.) We hear of a rule of private prayer three times a day, practiced by Daniel (Chapter 6:10; cf. Psalm 55:18). There is no doubt that the use of the sacred books in the synagogue had very much to do with the formation of the canon of Scripture. The synagogue existed in order to train up the people in the knowledge of the Book of the Faith.

Let us pause for a moment to notice that the beginning of the synagogue marked another great stage in the history of the Faith. It was a new thing in the history of religion for houses to be built in which the people should worship God and hear His word. In old Israel, as in other

ancient nations, the people were never allowed inside the
Temple building itself. It was built to house the sacred
Ark, as temples in other countries were built to house the
image of a god, and also as a store-house for the offer-
ings that were made; but the people stood round the
altar, in the open air. The synagogue, as a building provided with benches and a pulpit, was a new thing. Our
churches are still synagogues, with benches and pulpits,
and they carry on the functions of the synagogue, praise
and prayer, the reading of the Bible and the exposition of
it; they contain in addition a receptacle to hold a little of
the River Jordan (the font), and the Table of the Lord's
Supper.

During the exile the sacred writings of old Israel,
which had been written and preserved largely in the
"schools of the prophets" (2 Kings 2:3, etc.) were edited
and largely added to. The five Books of the Law assumed
something like their present shape. It was not that the old
records were put together for historical purposes, according to our modern notion; they were put together for
use, as the documents of the Faith, containing the great
story of God's mighty works in the past, which every
Israelite must know: the Exodus, the Covenant, the Law,
the Conquest of Canaan, together with what we called
the preface and the introduction. They were needed
then for use in the synagogue; they would be needed
when the great return to Palestine took place, and the
Lord returned to dwell in the midst of His people. It is
from that point of view that we must understand the
elaborate description of the Tabernacle in the wilderness
in Exodus 25-30; it is the Tabernacle that is described,
but it is the restored Temple that was in mind.

Several groups of exiles returned to Palestine; the

first probably about 538 B.C., and some more about 520, when Haggai and Zechariah prophesied and the Temple was rebuilt. In 444 Nehemiah returned and rebuilt the fortifications of Jerusalem; and probably about 50 years later (as scholars now seem to agree) came Ezra the scribe. Ezra was a great figure, around whose name all sorts of legends gathered in later days; and there is no doubt that he was the founder of the later Judaism, the Judaism which we know from the New Testament. In Nehemiah 8-10 there is a description of a great occasion when Ezra read to the assembled people in Jerusalem large parts of the Book of the Law, and the Levites expounded it. In Nehemiah 9 there follows a solemn liturgical prayer, in which God is praised for His dealings with Israel in the past, and Israel's sin is confessed; finally prayer is made for deliverance from the then present distress, and a solemn Covenant is made to observe the Law (Nehemiah 9:38 through Chapter 10). That, it seems, was none other than the full inauguration of the priestly Law which was in force in our Lord's day, and the foundation of the post-exilic reformed Judaism. The date may have been 397 B.C.

Thus begins another period in the history of the Faith: that of Israel under the Law. Of political history there is none till the time of the Maccabees; the nation was subject to the Persian Empire till 331 B.C. (when the Greek king Alexander the Great conquered the East) and after that to the Greek rulers of Syria and Egypt. About 170 B.C. Antiochus Epiphanes attempted to establish a uniform Greek culture throughout the entire Middle East (I Maccabees 1:41-42); his plan demanded universal tolerance of pagan religions, but could not tolerate the Israelite's exclusive worship of one God. The faithful remnant in Israel refused to forsake its faith and its traditions, and there were many martyrs (I Maccabees 1:63; 2:29-38); the Book of Daniel belongs to this time, and the three who refused to worship Nebuchadnezzar's golden image and were cast into the burning fiery furnace were really the witnesses for the Faith in the days of Antiochus (Daniel 3). It appeared then how good the work of the synagogues had been, in training up the people in faithfulness to God. Then came the heroic rising under Judas Maccabeus, which won for Israel a period of political independence, till the country was absorbed in the Roman Empire in the course of the first century B.C.

The period, then, was one in which Israel, set in the midst of a pagan world, jealously had to guard the integrity of its faith and spiritual life. Its faith stood, as of old, on the mighty works of God in the redemption of the people from Egypt and His Covenant with Israel; it had been purified and disciplined through suffering, and there was no more idolatry; but the whole main emphasis had come to be the observance of the Law. The typical expression of its piety is the wonderful Psalm 119, in which the Israelite gives voice to an ordered, disciplined and whole-hearted obedience to God's will, as set forth in His law and His testimonies, His statutes and His judgments. The first eight chapters of Proverbs show how necessary it was to guard against the corrupting influences of paganism with its lax morality.

There was loss, however, as well as gain. Something was missing in that careful, rigid, zealous Judaism of the Law, with its emphasis on the rules of ritual purity and the exact observance of the Sabbath. It had its great virtues of religious conscientiousness and a high moral standard, but there were no more prophets, and the prophetic spirit seemed to disappear. The glorious hopes of the Second Isaiah and many psalms, that the Faith was to be proclaimed to all nations, and that Israel held it in trust for them, had for the time being dropped almost out of sight in the Judaism of Palestine.

The reason was this: that hope of the evangelization of the Gentiles depended on the fulfilment of the promise of the return of the Lord's Presence to dwell among His people, the outpouring of the Spirit, and the inauguration of the New Covenant; and that had not happened. God's time was not yet come. He was keeping His people waiting, keeping them under the discipline of the Law, to learn its lessons and to be trained up in the ways of a disciplined spiritual life. Thus, for the time being, though the Temple had been restored and the sacrifices were offered with carefulness and on the whole not without devotion, one important element in Israel's religion was missing; there were no prophets in the last two or three centuries before our Lord.

The time came, however, when there appeared in Israel men whose faces were radiant with joy, proclaiming that God's time had come, and all had been fulfilled in Jesus, of the seed of David, the promised Messiah. We now come to our third confession of faith*, by a disciple of Jesus the Christ: "It was all true. God redeemed His people of old from Egypt, made His Covenant with us, gave us the Law, brought us into the promised land. God spoke later by His prophets, who announced a second Exodus, a New Covenant, a gift of the Spirit, a return of the Presence, the preaching of the

*I owe the idea of the three confessions of faith to W. J. Phythian-Adams. *The Idea of At-one-ment,* (1944) pages 24-26.

Gospel to all nations. It all has happened and is happening before our eyes. God has visited and redeemed His people, not from Egypt nor from the north country, but from the whole power of the Enemy of mankind, from Satan, sin, and death, by the death and resurrection of the Lord Jesus. He has inaugurated the New Covenant in His blood. The Spirit was poured out at Pentecost, and is active in our midst. The Presence has returned; the Word was made flesh, and tabernacled among us, and we beheld His glory. And now we see the Gospel being proclaimed to the Greek on the same terms as to the Jew, and people of all nations admitted to share in the privilege of membership in the Israel of God, and we look for a glorious future in which, under the conditions of the world to come, the salvation which has come to us here and now in this world will be made complete, through His second Advent, in His eternal and glorious Kingdom."

Here we have the fulfilment of the Old Testament, and the completion of the sacred history.

CHAPTER IV

The New Testament Fulfilment

Our third confession of faith has been given as a summary of the teaching of the New Testament. The books of the New Testament contain the testimony of the Apostles to the events of the second Redemption, and their teaching about the Christian way of life; and it was as the apostolic books that they were accepted by the Church, and put together with the Jewish Scriptures to form the Christian Bible. The list of New Testament books was substantially complete by the end of the second century, though it was not finally settled till the fourth century.

"Think not that I came to destroy the law or the prophets: I came not to destroy but to fulfil" (Matthew 5:17). Everything in the New Testament is based on the Old. St. Mark records the first words of our Lord's ministry as, "The time is fulfilled and the kingdom of God is at hand: repent ye, and believe the gospel" (Mark 1:15)—that is, the glad tidings that the Kingdom or Reign of God announced by the Prophets has now come. The very words "Jesus Christ" imply the Kingdom: for "Christ" is the Greek word for the Hebrew "Messiah", which means "The Anointed One"—that is, the promised King anointed or consecrated to His royal office by the Holy Ghost, who descended on Him at His baptism.

Thence it was and still is impossible to explain who Jesus was and what He had come to do, except in terms of the Old Testament. He came to be King Messiah (Luke 23:2), and it was for His Kingship that He was

45

crucified; He died with the title "The King of the Jews" nailed up over His head. He was and is King, however, in the sense of being King over God's Kingdom, and not as one of the kings of this world, exercising temporal power; for had it been so, His servants would have had to bear arms and fight, that He should not be delivered to the Jews (John 18:36). His Kingdom was, and is, of a different order from that. He is King, in God's Name, over men's hearts and consciences, because He is come "to bear witness unto the truth", to the truth of God and God's rule over men, and "every one that is of the truth" hears His voice (John 18:37).

It was because He was King in that sense that He entered Jerusalem on Palm Sunday, riding not on a war-horse but on an ass, with the prophecy of Zechariah in mind: "Rejoice greatly, O daughter of Zion . . . behold, thy King cometh unto thee . . . lowly, and riding upon an ass . . . .And I will cut off the chariot from Ephraim, and the horse from Jerusalem, and the battle-bow shall be cut off. And he shall speak peace unto the nations; and his dominion shall be from sea to sea, and from the river to the ends of the earth" (Zechariah 9:9-10). Indeed, at the very beginning, in His tempta-tion on the Mount, the issue had been settled once for all; to have sought "the kingdoms of this world and the glory of them" would have been to surrender to the Devil at the start, and to renounce the spiritual kingdom which He had come to set up (Matthew 4:8-11).

No prophecies from the Old Testament are more con-stantly quoted in the New than those of the Servant of the Lord in Second Isaiah. Not only are they used of Him by the apostolic writers, as in Matthew 12:18-21 or Acts 8:32-35; He Himself accepted them as giving the very central meaning of His ministry, which reached its climax in His "giving his life a ransom for many" (Mark 10:45) and His acceptance of a sacrificial death for the sake of the divine Kingdom. "It was written" that He should suffer (Mark 9:12; 14:21, 27, 49); and there were not only the direct predictions which the prophets had made, but also the fact that they and the other servants of God had shown by their own sufferings that the way of suffering was God's royal road (Matthew 21:35-36; 23:34-36). We saw in the last chapter how the mark of the Cross lies across the Old Testament as well as the New.

So it worked out in the Lord's own life: He came among men announcing the Kingdom or Kingly Rule of God; that is the theme of one parable after another. Of that Kingdom He is the King; He is the Sower who comes sowing the seed of God's word, and the Shepherd who will gather together the Lord's flock; He comes to Jerusalem longing to gather her children together like a hen gathering her chickens under her wing; He is the King's Son, who calls the people of Israel to the marriage-feast which God has provided for Him. He is the Messiah of the reconstituted Israel in which the people of all nations are to find their home. In His teaching He set before His disciples and the multitudes in the plainest terms the spiritual demand of the divine Kingdom. It meant not mere obedience to the precepts of the Law, as the Scribes interpreted it, but an entire self-surrender to God; it meant renouncing not merely the sins of the flesh and other transgressions of the Ten Commandments, but also of self-righteousness which, in the last resort, is a worship of the self and a refusal to worship God.

No one could deny the high moral tone of His teach-

ing; but the leaders of the nation felt that it was alto-
gether too much of a good thing. It was intolerable that
He should criticize in that way the respectable religion
of good-living people, and call the righteous Pharisees
hypocrites. They dared not face up to it. As He Himself
put it, they said in their hearts, "We will not have this
man to reign over us" (Luke 19:14). They were indeed
looking for the advent of their Messiah; but they wanted
a Messiah who would render a proper respect to the well-
intentioned religion of good people. Very many were
ready to follow one who would claim temporal power
and organize a holy war against the Roman government,
but a Messiah, who brought the claim of God's rule over
men so uncomfortably near, and who believed that by
His word God could even there and then forgive sins
(Mark 2:10), was asking of them too much. When by
claiming authority over the Temple and expelling the
traders from the Court of the Gentiles (Mark 11:15-18)
He forced them to say Yes or No to the one question that
mattered, the chief priests finally made up their minds
that there must be an end to it: that man was not God's
Messiah but an accursed pretender.

There was and is only one question at issue between
the Lord Jesus and all who believe in Him on the one
hand, and the Jews and the world at large on the other.
It is not the question of the nobility of His character or
of the teaching of the Sermon on the Mount; there is no
question about that. It is the question whether He really
was the promised Christ; whether in Him the Lord God
of Israel has visited and redeemed His people; whether
He is the Son of God and the Saviour of the world—or
whether His Gospel was false, and God was *not* in Him
visiting and redeeming His people; in which case, it

would follow that He Himself had totally misconceived His mission. That and that alone is the question; and every man must say for himself whether he acknowledges Jesus as the Messiah and the Son of God, and accepts also the spiritual demand which that involves on himself, or is content that Jesus should be crucified.

He went to His death in the faith that through Him God was redeeming Israel His people. God's hour had come, in which the divine Reign foretold by the Prophets was being established, in which the New Covenant announced by Jeremiah was being inaugurated. Because of the sin of man, because of the sin, above all, of self-righteousness, it could happen only through sacrifice, through the martyrdom of the Servant of the Lord who should "bear the sins of many" and his soul be made "a sacrifice for sin"; therefore, "before the feast of the passover, Jesus, knowing that the hour was come in which he should depart out of this world unto the Father, having loved his own which were in the world, he loved them to the uttermost" (John 13:1), and at the Last Supper added to the familiar ritual of the supper-meal some words in which He designated the broken bread as His body, and the cup of wine at the end of the meal as "the new covenant in my blood" (1 Corinthians 11: 25). "My blood" meant "my sacrifice": by that sacrifice the New Covenant was being ratified, the New Covenant which was to be written in men's hearts, bringing them to true knowledge of God and forgiveness of sin. And His disciples were to "do this" afterwards for His remembrance: that is to say, when they took bread according to His ordinance and blessed and broke it, it would be His sacrificed Body, and their cup would be His Blood of the New Covenant; He would be in their midst as Mes-

siah-King and Priest and Sacrifice, as the Christ whom
men had rejected and God had vindicated. That is the
meaning of the Resurrection and Ascension, as given by
St. Peter at Pentecost: "ye by the hands of law-less men
did crucify and slay" Him; "God raised him up", and
"God hath made him both Lord and Christ" (Acts 2:23-
24, 36). At every Eucharist, therefore, the Church answers the question of all questions with a triumphant
Yes.

The Apostles state the answer, and the Church still
states it, in Old Testament terms, corresponding to the
several points of messianic hope. The second Redemption is another Exodus, but this time we have been delivered not from Egypt nor from Babylon, but from the
evil power which at the fall of Man corrupted our human
nature and dragged it to ruin along the road that led to
death; by His resurrection we have passed from death
unto life. Christ is our Passover who is sacrificed for us;
therefore at Easter and at every Eucharist we keep the
paschal feast, not with the old leaven, nor with the leaven
of malice and wickedness like Caiaphas' Passover on the
night of the first Good Friday (cf. John 18:28), but
with the unleavened bread of sincerity and truth (I Corinthians 5:7-8). The New Covenant is written "not in
tables of stone, but in tables that are hearts of flesh"; it
has its appointed ministers but it is not another Law,
since it is not of the letter that killeth but of the Spirit
who gives life (2 Corinthians 3:3-6). The love of God
has been shed abroad in our hearts through the Spirit
who was given to us (Romans 5:5). The return of the
Presence of the Lord has taken place: "the Word was
made flesh, and dwelt (tabernacled) among us" (John
1:14). Of old, it had been a Presence in the midst of

Israel: "I will walk *among* you, and will be your God, and ye shall be my people" (Leviticus 26:12) ; such was the Presence of the Lord among men in the days of His flesh, and such is His Presence in His holy Sacrament; but the words of St. John, "dwelt among us" can also be translated "dwelt in us"; and St. Paul thus quotes the text from Leviticus, "We are a temple of the living God, even as God said, I dwell *in* them and walk *in* them, and I will be their God and they shall be my people" (2 Corinthians 6:16). The true Temple of God now is built of living stones (1 Peter 2:5) ; "the Church", in the proper sense, is not the building but the people.

The last point in the messianic hope was that all nations should come to the knowledge of Israel's God. St. Paul shows how the hope had been fulfilled. In the eyes of the law-abiding Jew, and in his own eyes when he had been Saul the Pharisee, the Gentile was an outsider, a sinner; but the Lord Jesus had shown that the righteous Pharisee was a sinner too, and all the more a sinner because of his self-righteousness (that had been proved up to the hilt when the righteous Jews had joined in crucifying Him, the Holy One of God) ; but in His sacrifice for sin and His resurrection God's love had been victorious over man's sin, and therefore there was forgiveness and mercy for all: for the self-righteous Pharisee and the unrighteous Gentile alike and on the same terms. "God hath shut up all unto disobedience, that he might have mercy upon all" (Romans 11:32). "There can be neither Jew nor Greek, there can neither bond nor free, there can be no male and female"—the diversities of race and status and sex indeed remain, but they are reconciled—"for ye are all one man in Christ Jesus" (Galatians 3:28).

So the Old Testament imagery all comes back, but on a higher level. The Law and the Prophets are fulfilled, not destroyed; but they are made new in Him "who maketh all things new". Our Lord is King, but He is no temporal monarch. He is our high priest, not of the same order as Caiaphas, but "holy, guileless, undefiled, separated from sinners, and made higher than the heavens" (Hebrews 7:26), the "priest for ever after the order of Melchizedek" (Hebrews 5:6-10). All the Old Testament sacrificial ritual is seen to be fulfilled in His one sacrifice; and the rubrics of the Day of Atonement which we read in Leviticus 16:16-17, take on a new meaning: "he shall make atonement for the holy place, because of the uncleannesses of the children of Israel . . . and there shall be no man in the tent of meeting when he goeth in to make atonement for the holy place, until he come out, and have made atonement."

The very fact that the Old Testament promises are fulfilled in Christ makes it necessary that the Old Testament imagery should thus receive a mystical or spiritual interpretation. Such an interpretation is given to them throughout the New Testament; there is nothing arbitrary or fanciful about it, since it all follows straight from the fulfilment of the several points of the messianic hope. Neither is it a meaning imposed afterwards by the Apostles on the events of the Gospel story; it goes back to our Lord Himself, and it is all implied in His action at the Last Supper, when He interpreted His death as the sacrifice for sin. Of the two earliest accounts, that of St. Paul in I Corinthians 11 refers directly, as we have seen, to the prophecy of the New Covenant in Jeremiah, in the words "This cup is the new covenant in my blood"; while the corresponding words in Mark 14:24, "This is my blood of the covenant", refer directly to the words of Moses at the ratification of the Old Covenant at Sinai, "Behold the blood of the covenant which the Lord hath made with you" (Exodus 24:8).

Here, then, we have a principle of 'spiritual interpretation" which depends on the necessary connection of the New Testament fulfilment with the Old Testament type. Almost without exception the use made of the Old Testament in the liturgy of the Church faithfully follows the line which the New Testament writers have marked out. We shall have more to say about the matter in the last chapter but one.

It is necessary to distinguish the legitimate and necessary spiritual interpretation from the somewhat fanciful and arbitrary "allegorical interpretations" which have often been given. One of which the Fathers are very fond is the interpretation of the scarlet cord which Rahab hung from her window on the wall of Jericho, that she and her household might be saved when the city was destroyed (Joshua 2:18-21), as typifying the blood of Christ by which we are saved from the condemnation of the sinful world. It is a thought that we too can find helpful, and it ought not to be called "wrong", but it lies right off the direct line of connection between the Old Testament and the New; it is a poetical fancy, connecting the color red with "salvation".

St. Paul and other New Testament writers sometimes use the Old Testament in a similar way, as in the oft-quoted passage about Hagar and Sarah which comes in the Epistle for the Fourth Sunday in Lent (Galatians 4:21-31). There, however, St. Paul was giving an interpretation after the manner of the Jewish rabbis to his Galatian readers who were clamoring for rabbinic inter-

pretations, to show that, if it came to that, he too could
allegorize. Or again, in Ephesians 4:7-11, where he is
speaking of the gift of the apostolic ministry to the
Church by the ascended Christ, he uses a text from
Psalms 68, "When he ascended up on high, he led cap-
tivity captive, and gave gifts unto men". That does not
follow directly from the original meaning of the psalm,
which is speaking of a victorious king, perhaps David,
going up to Jerusalem with the prisoners whom he has
captured. It is obvious that the text from the psalm did
not give St. Paul his authority for saying that Christ had
instituted the apostolic ministry; he was simply borrow-
ing Old Testament language to express something which
he believed to be true on other grounds. It was only a
convenient illustration and it shows clearly the distinction between such a use of the Old Testament and the
true and proper spiritual interpretation, which depends
on the fact that certain things had happened in the history
of Israel, and certain things had been said by the Prophets, which had been fulfilled in the events of the second
Redemption.

Such a true comparison is the one St. Paul makes in
I Corinthians 10 (which we read in the Epistle for the
Ninth Sunday after Trinity), between the condition of
his Corinthian Christians and that of Israel in the wilderness. "Our fathers were under the cloud, and all
passed through the sea, and were all baptized unto Moses
in the cloud and in the sea, and did all eat the same spiritual meat, and drank of the same spiritual drink", yet
through their sin were overthrown in the wilderness, and
were not allowed to enter the promised land (I Corinthians 10:1-6). He is saying: You Corinthians have en-
joyed the blessings of the second Redemption; you have

dwelt in the divine Presence, under the pillar of cloud, you have been through the Red Sea in your baptism, and in your Eucharist you partake of the manna and of the water from the Rock: therefore, beware; as the Israelites who sinned of old in the wilderness failed to enter into the promised land, so will you, if you lust and commit idolatry and tempt the Lord and murmur against Him. You have still to cross your Jordan and enter the land that flows with milk and honey.

In one sense, we, like St. Paul's Corinthians, are on the way to the promised land; in another, we have already entered it. Both things are true at once. We are pilgrims on the way to Jerusalem, or we are exiles in Babylon, looking forward to our return thither; yet also, we are already there, and are citizens of the Jerusalem which is above and is free and is the Mother of us all. On Good Friday, we stand before the Cross and are accused of sin; but our Easter communion means that we are risen with Christ and our life is even now hid with Christ in God. We are members of Christ, new-born to eternal life; yet there is still in us the Old Adam, needing to be fought and overcome in detail. We are members on earth of the Kingdom of Christ; but we also look forward to the second Advent and the life of the world to come, when the divine work of salvation, which is already complete as regards Christ, will have been made complete in us. The Messiah has come, He has offered His sacrifice, and has established the divine Reign on earth among men; but we, the members of the Church militant on earth, are still incomplete and imperfect; and it is in the future world, to which we look forward, that God's work of salvation will have been made complete in the Church triumphant.

CHAPTER V

THE BIBLE AS HISTORY

IN the last three chapters we have tried to gain a view of the Bible as a whole. It tells a story covering a period of some twenty centuries, from Abraham and Moses to St. John the Divine. The story is that of the sacred history: that is, the working out in history of God's purpose of salvation for mankind. The preface to the Bible gives the setting of the story: the world is God's world which He has created, and man, His creature, has been put in it that he may live his life to God's glory; but man has sinned, and the world has become a dark and sinful world. The introduction to the Bible tells of the beginning of His saving purpose in the promise to Abraham. The main story consists of God's choice of Israel to be His people, and of His dealing with Israel through fifteen centuries, culminating in the coming of God Himself to save mankind, and of the re-constituting of Israel as the Church of all the nations.

Such a view of the Bible clears up at once some of the difficulties which are felt about it. God's choice of Israel to be His own people does not mean that God had no care for the other nations of mankind, such as the Greeks and Romans, the Indians and the Chinese. On the contrary, it is emphasized from the start that God is the creator of the world and of all men. God had things to teach the other nations also. The prophet Amos says that as He had brought up Israel from the land of Egypt, so He had brought the Philistines from Caphtor and the Syrians from Kir (Amos 9:7). St. Paul, preaching to pagans at Lystra, says that among them also God has not left Himself without witness (Acts 14:17); in the Epistle to the Romans he says that the Gentiles have a real knowledge of God, so that in doing wrong they are guilty of sinning against Him (Romans 1:18-21), and when they obey their conscience and do right they show that they have His law written in their hearts (Romans 2:14-16). St. John speaks of the Word of God as the Light that lighteneth every man that cometh into the world (John 1:9). The prophets and the psalms are full of the hope that Israel's knowledge of the true God is held in trust for the people of all nations; and in the New Testament we see that hope in process of being fulfilled.

Further, if the Bible is God's book and is inspired, that does not mean that the Holy Ghost has ceased to speak and act since the last book of the Bible was written. On the contrary, the fact that the sacred history related in the Bible closes at the point at which God's purpose is completely worked out in the one nation of Israel, means that Church history is then about to begin. Church history is the continuation of the story; it tells of the works of the Holy Ghost in all the nations of the world, as they enter into the Church and come to share in the inheritance of Israel; therefore the last book of history in the Bible, the Acts of the Apostles, ends very significantly with the picture of the work of God going forward: St. Paul "abode two whole years in his own hired house, and received all that went in unto him, preaching the kingdom of God and teaching the things concerning the Lord Jesus Christ, with all boldness, none forbidding him (Acts 28:30-31). That work is still going on; and everywhere in the Church and among all Christians the Bible is put in a central place, as being the story of the inheritance of Israel on which all nations now enter.

We are now concerned with the Bible as history; the essential question is, Is the history true? Did God really thus reveal Himself in the events of the sacred history? Did He really visit and redeem His people? If the story told in the Bible is a true story, then it contains the true answer to the problem of the dark and sinful world in which we live, and of the meaning of our own lives. The question divides itself into two. Is the answer, taken as a whole, a true answer? And is the story, particularly at the crucial points, truly told, so that it will stand up to historical investigation and vindicate itself as true history?

First, then, let us look at the Bible as a whole. Look at it as the Book of the Faith in which the saints of God under both Covenants have believed. Read the eleventh chapter of the Epistle to the Hebrews, with its magnificent picture of the great procession of the saints of God through many generations, who lived their earthly lives by faith in the things not seen, looking always for "the city which hath foundations, whose builder and maker is God" (Hebrews 11:10), who "died in faith, not having received the promises, but having seen them and greeted them from afar, and having confessed that they were strangers and pilgrims on the earth" (verse 13); "wherefore God is not ashamed of them, to be called their God; for he hath prepared for them a city" (verse 16); "by faith Abraham . . . by faith Isaac . . . by faith Jacob . . . by faith Moses . . ." and all God's servants, "Who through faith subdued kingdoms, wrought righteousness, obtained promises, stopped the mouths of lions, escaped the edge of the sword, from weakness were made strong"; the martyrs "of whom the world was not

worthy, wandering in deserts and mountains and caves
and the holes of the earth" (verse 38); and we, who are
"compassed about with so great a cloud of witnesses",
are bidden to "run with patience the race that is set before us, looking unto Jesus the author (or captain) and
perfecter of [our] faith, who for the joy that was set
before him endured the cross, despising shame, and hath
sat down at the right hand of the throne of God" (Chapter 12:1-2). Since the day the Epistle was written, the
Church has been gathered out of all nations and tribes
and peoples and tongues, the martyrs and confessors and
the multitude, which no man can number, of simple believing Christians, who have lived and died in the faith,
and have triumphed over suffering and have gone to
their rest.

Next, let us confront with the testimony of the saints
of the old and the new Israel, the typical attitude of the
modern world which has drifted away from the Biblical
and Christian tradition, a world which is wonderfully
clever in scientific investigation and mechanical inven-
tion, but in all the things that matter most has lost its
sense of direction; it is zealous for education, but does
not know what is the education which it wants to give; it
has lost or is losing its moral standards, and men drift
aimlessly, with little sense of any real meaning or purpose
in their lives. The question is not, whether the Christian
faith or some rival belief is true; but rather, whether
faith is possible for man at all. It must be either the Christian Faith, as the Bible sets it forth, or nothing. "Lord, to
whom shall we go?"—there is nowhere else to go, there
is no other belief which can even begin to answer the
problem set by the life of man in this dark and sinful
world; therefore the Christian confession is, "Thou hast

the words of eternal life." In Christ there is the answer
which meets the need, but there needs also to be the
personal self-commitment of each believer: "We believe
and know that thou art the Holy One of God" (John
6:68-69).

Such is the Faith of the Bible in the context of the
modern world: the Faith to which the saints of God under both Covenants bear witness. The writers of the Biblical books—lawgivers, prophets, psalmists, apostles,
evangelists—are our fathers in the Faith, sharers with
us in one hope, united in one bond of love in the communion of saints, in the blessed company of all faithful
people, in the mystical body of Christ our Lord. The
truth of the Faith depends on the truth of the story
which the Bible tells, of the working out in history of
God's saving purpose.

We come then to the second part of our question:
Does the story, especially at the crucial points, stand up
to historical investigation and vindicate itself as true
history? The crucial points are the decisive events of the
first and the second Redemptions, at which our Faith
proclaims that God's arm was bared: the Exodus, when
God delivered His people out of Egypt and made His
Covenant with them, and the self-offering of our Lord
in sacrifice for man's salvation, and the vindication of
His sacrifice by the act of God in raising Him from the
dead on the third day. As regards the first Redemption,
the question is whether the faith of the prophets and
people of Israel rested on a true tradition of an action of
God, or whether the Exodus-story was a mere myth, and
so the faith of Israel rested on illusion and not on truth.
As regards the second Redemption, the question is
whether our Lord really believed Himself to be the Mes-

siah and the Servant of the Lord whom Second Isaiah
foretold, or if that whole interpretation of His life-work
was imposed afterwards on the events by the Apostles;
and whether the evidence for the resurrection of His
body vindicates itself as truthful evidence, or can be
proved to be a legend which sprang up later. St. Paul is
quite clear that the point is crucial: "If Christ hath not
been raised, your faith in vain; ye are yet in your sins",
since in that case the Gospel message of the divine Kingdom and the forgiveness of sins is baseless; it rests on a
falsehood, because (in that case) "we (Apostles) are
found false witnesses of God, because we witnessed of
God that he raised up Christ" (I Corinthians 15:14-17).

At this point the writer of this book is confronted with
a difficulty. We are bound to say that the historical truth
of the story of the Exodus in the Old Testament, and that
of our Lord's Resurrection in the New, are essential to
the Faith; but in a book of this size it is impossible to
discuss those questions properly. One can give reasons,
as for instance that the stories of the Exodus and the
wilderness-period are attested not only by the actual
narratives, but by very many allusions in the historical
books (e.g. Judges 6:13), the prophets (e.g. Amos 3:1),
and the psalms (e.g. Psalm 77:15, 20), and by the Song
of Miriam in Exodus 15 (which is very ancient indeed,
much older than the prose narrative), and further by the
existence of the Ark, the Tent of Meeting or Tabernacle,
and the Passover; but a serious attempt to give the
reasons as they ought to be given would require a spe-
cialist inquiry, using technical language, and therefore
as difficult to the "layman" as an exposition of the atomic
theory, couched in professional terms which most of us
find extremely hard to follow.

Respect for the seriousness of historical study forbids
us from trying to do in a few pages a task which demands
a book to itself, but what we can usefully do is to point
out how seriously the Church takes the appeal of the
Faith to historical fact, by the extraordinarily thorough
and painstaking work that is devoted to Biblical scholarship. The Faith is challenged by unbelieving critics. The
Church takes up the challenge, and is prepared to see the
matter through, facing all possible tests. A debt of grati-
tude is owed to the scholars who have approached the
study of Biblical problems with critical minds, full
equipment of training and knowledge, and at the same
time as Christian believers, and have found that the foundations of their faith stand firm. It is enheartening
that the Church has not shirked the challenge of Biblical
criticism. There need be no fear of the result.

The central point of all is the faith that God has visited
and redeemed His people, and the redemption has taken
place in events of history. If the story of God's redemptive action were to be demonstrated to be myth or legend,
the rest of the Biblical history would be of no particular
interest. The Apostles, however, stood before the world
as "witnesses of the resurrection" (Acts 1:22; 3:15;
10:41); they appealed to the facts of history; and the
Church today, with the use of modern critical methods,
carries on the same testimony. When therefore that
testimony is shown to stand firm at the crucial points,
there is nothing else to cause any anxiety in the rest of
the Biblical history. No one doubts, for instance, that
the main substance of the Books of Samuel and Kings,
or of the life of St. Paul as narrated in the Acts of the
Apostles, is substantially correct; if there is uncertainty
about minor points, we can be content to let the his-

torians worry about such matters.

As for the stories which come in the preface to the Bible, those of the creation of the world, of the Garden of Eden, and of the Flood, we can be content to recognize that the writers of those stories were deliberately using the language of myth, as the only possible language in which to convey the essential truths which they intended to convey about God and the world, about the true place of man in God's world, and about the ruin which man has brought upon himself by his sin. Such was the account which we gave of these stories in an earlier chapter (see pages 24-26 above). The writers were not writing history, on the basis of historical memories, as were, for instance, the writers of the records of the reigns of David and Solomon. They were not concerned with the scientific truth of the material evolution of our planet, as are modern writers on astronomy, geology, biology and anthropology, but with truth on a higher level, the truth about the world and human life in relation to God; and that, after all, is what we go to the Bible for.

Much confusion at this point has been caused by the "fundamentalist" doctrine, that if the Bible is true, and is God's book, it must be free from all error at every possible point. Either, it is said, the Bible is inspired and everything in it is literally true; or, if some things in it are not literally true, it cannot be God's Book. That sort of fundamentalism, at least in its modern form, involves a strange surrender to the materialism of the day, which assumes that the only real truth of things is the truth of material fact and history. On such a view, the true picture of a thing is that which the camera reveals, not what the painter sees in it; and poetry becomes an imaginative embroidery of the facts, possessing little real value. Thus the biblical accounts themselves become strangely materialized; the ascension of our Lord is taken to mean the translation of His physical body to the stratosphere; but the Bible says that He ascended into heaven, and sat on the right hand of the Father; and that is a very different thing.

The nemesis of the false assumption of fundamentalism is that people draw the opposite conclusion to that which is intended. The fundamentalist Christian intends to assert that the Bible is God's book, and comes to us with the authority of His word; and that is true, but he makes the false inference that everything in it must therefore be "literally" true. The ordinary person, realizing that there are things in the Bible which are not "literally" true, draws the opposite conclusion, that the Bible is not God's book, and can be set aside; for him, the Bible is a fallen oracle.

It is that view which forms a main cause of confusion in the popular mind today. The story of Adam and Eve, people say, is not true; it is a mere fable. The rest of the Bible is dismissed in the same way, and not taken seriously. It seems to belong to a different world of thought from our own. The Christmas story is very popular; but multitudes of people think of it as something like a fairy-tale, and the Christmas cards, with pretty angels and the romantic surroundings of the stable, reinforce the impression. They do not reckon with the serious fact that the Son of God was made man for us men and for our salvation.

Here we are back at one of the crucial points of God's action in history; it is interesting therefore to find a tendency in modern religious art (to which there are parallels in early medieval art) deliberately to avoid the cult of "prettiness". It was into this dark and sinful world of ours that the Son of God came when He was made man; and that fact is emphasized by the Church, which keeps as festivals in the days immediately after Christmas the martyrdom of St. Stephen and the murder of the Holy Innocents.

It is necessary to hold fast to the truth of God's saving purpose in history, which the Bible relates. In so doing, the Christian today cannot take the too easy and simple way of fundamentalism. It is not true that the Bible is free from all possible error; God did not intend to teach us through it the sort of truth which He has left us to learn through our study of astronomy, geology, and the other sciences, but the far more fundamental truth of His purpose to redeem our sinful world. That truth is given in the history of His dealings with the nation which He chose to be His people.

Fundamentalism makes another error; it misses the important truth that God's method of redemption has been to reveal Himself through men. Necessarily, therefore, the books of the Bible bear the marks of the imperfection of their human writers, who tell us the story of God's wonderful dealings with them; they write always in the light of their faith in the living God. In narrative, prophecy and psalm they endeavor to trace the ways of His working and to learn His will. In the next chapter we shall have to see how the true lessons which imperfect men were engaged in learning throughout the Old Testament are gathered up and made complete in the final and perfect revelation of God in His Son.

In this chapter we have been occupied with the truth of the Bible as history. The key to the truth of the Bible as history lies, as we have sufficiently seen, in the crucial events of the two Redemptions, on which the whole story hinges, and on the truth of which the faith of the Bible and of the Church depends.

Therefore it is that in the daily lessons at Morning and Evening Prayer we read the Bible through in order, the greater part of the Old Testament once, and the New Testament mostly twice, in the course of the year; while at the great festivals we celebrate the crucial events of the Redemption which form the climax of the story. It often seems difficult to find much matter for edification in the Old Testament lessons; many parts of the narrative seem to have little directly to teach us; yet it is profoundly impressive to contemplate the long succession of generations which succeeded one another, and think how the divine purpose is slowly moving to its climax in the advent of the Messiah. Sometimes we get a glimpse of that majestic progress, as at the end of the Book of Ruth, we read that a child was born to Ruth, and "they called his name Obed; he is the father of Jesse, the father of David" (Ruth 4:17).

CHAPTER VI

THE BIBLE TEACHING

OUR sketch of the Old Testament history in the second and third chapters of this book showed how throughout the history a continuous spiritual development was going on. The God who acted decisively in the events of the Redemption was present and active in the whole course of the history, educating His people in the true knowledge of Himself and the way of His spiritual service. After Israel had been chosen and called to be the people of God, it had to learn what the service of God meant, and what it cost. All through the history, imperfect men were being trained up as pupils in the divine school, and were learning the lessons which He had to teach them. We must not be surprised if they did not learn the lessons all at once; but God was teaching them, and they gained insights of truth which were always incomplete, but nevertheless real. The Prophets spoke God's word; but no prophet, not even the greatest, was able to see the whole vision of God's purpose. It was only when the Son of God came that God's word was heard, full and complete. Jesus Christ not only speaks God's word, but personally is that Word. In Him, in His teaching, His person, His life-work, His death and resurrection, God's final Word is spoken to men.

Such general considerations help to throw light on the problem of the inspiration of the Bible. When we say that the Bible is "inspired", we mean that God inspired it, God spoke His word through the human writer. But what was the word which God had to say? It cannot

be simply identified with the words spoken by Isaiah or
Jeremiah; for their vision of God's purpose was, as we
have said, true but imperfect. The word which God had
to speak, the teaching which He had to convey to men, is
that which is given in the whole course of the sacred
history, and summed up in the person and the work of
Jesus Christ; therefore, we need always to think of the
whole Old Testament as leading up to Him, as fulfilled
and made complete in Him. We must read back the New
Testament into the Old, and see the Old Testament in
the light of the New.

To illustrate: it is the teaching of the Book of Deuteronomy that if the people walk in God's ways, they will
receive God's blessing and it will be well with them; if
they disobey Him, they will deserve His punishment
(see *e.g.* Deuteronomy 28:1-14, and 15-end). That became the accepted teaching; we find it for instance in
Psalm 37, which we read on the seventh evening of the
month. But is it true? Certainly it is true in the long run
that well-doing receives its reward; but is it true in every
particular case? In the Book of Job the accepted doctrine
is expressed in the speeches of Job's three friends, but is
vigorously criticized by Job himself. The poems of the
Servant of the Lord in Second Isaiah similarly show the
Servant of the Lord as enduring present suffering, but
as vindicated by God at the last. It is that view of the
matter which is shown to be right by the crucifixion and
resurrection of our Lord.

Again: animal sacrifices are commanded in the Law;
throughout the history, except during the exile when
sacrifices were impossible, they form the central feature
of Israel's worship; yet again and again prophets and
psalmists criticize the sacrifices. In very many places

they are indeed condemning, not the sacrifices themselves, but the people who offer them in the wrong spirit,
as if by offering sacrifices they could buy God's favor.
Thus Isaiah, in Chapter 1:10-17, condemns the sacrifices which the people are offering and not those only,
but also their sabbaths and assemblies, their appointed
feasts and their prayers; it is the people who are wrong,
and are profaning the holy observances of their religion
by their impenitent lives. "Wash you, make you clean;
put away the evil of your doings from before mine eyes;
cease to do evil; learn to do well" (verses 16-17). There
are other places in which the prophets see, not only that
God wants man's love and obedience—"Behold, to obey
is better than sacrifice, and to hearken than the fat of
rams" (1 Samuel 15:22)—but also that God has no
need of animal sacrifices: "Thinkest thou that I will
eat bulls' flesh, and drink the blood of goats?" (Psalm
50:13). Sometimes it is roundly said: "Burnt-offerings,
and sacrifice for sin, hast thou not required; then said I,
Lo I come; in the volume of the book it is written of me,
that I should fulfil thy will, O my God' (Psalm 40:9-
10, and see Hebrews 10:5-10). One psalmist goes
further, to see that the *real* meaning of the sacrifice of
the animal is that it is a symbol of the sacrifice of man
himself: "The sacrifice of God is a troubled spirit; a
broken and contrite heart, O God, shalt thou not despise"
(Psalm 51:17); and it is in that sense that Second
Isaiah says of the Servant of the Lord that his soul is
made "a sacrifice for sin" (Isaiah 53:10). Thus the Old
Testament, at the point of its very deepest insight, antici-
pates that sacrificial offering which the son of God
Himself made.

It was in such ways that the spiritual development

of Israel in the Old Testament led up to our Lord, and
was made complete in Him. We will now see how that
principle throws light on the prayers for vengeance on
enemies, which we find in several of the psalms and elsewhere in the Old Testament, notably in the saintly prophet Jeremiah (Chapter 11:18-20; 17:18). We noticed in
the first chapter what difficulty such references cause
to many today.

The conflict against the Lord's enemies is a theme
which runs through the whole Bible; but the question
which constantly arises is, who the Lord's enemies really
are. In the early part of the history, they were identified
with the enemies of Israel; there was continual warfare
against the Amorites and other tribes; the Israelites as a
nation were at a stage corresponding to adolescence in
the individual, and, like boys, they were often thought-
lessly cruel. The ballad of Deborah in Judges, Chapter 5,
is perhaps the oldest poem in the Bible, and in it Jael the
wife of Heber the Kenite shows a devoted zeal for the
Lord's cause; but her ideas of the way in which the
Lord's battle should be fought are not exactly a model
for our imitation. Sisera was the Lord's enemy; he had
to be struck down. Saul, a little later, went to fight the
Amalekites; he had to destroy them. David fought Go-
liath; and that deservedly popular story, splendidly told
in 1 Samuel 17, has remained for us as a pattern of the
conflict of the champion of the Lord's cause against
swaggering, insolent powers of evil, far superior in
brute strength.

As time went on, however, simple identification of the
Lord's enemies with the enemies of Israel became impossible. The prophets accused Israel of sin, and de-
clared that the Lord Himself was sending the enemies of

Israel against them for their chastisement (see *e.g.* Isaiah 10:5-6). It was then not so easy to say who were the Lord's enemies, but certainly the people in Israel who provoked His wrath were the sinners who profaned His worship, who went after other gods, who oppressed His poor; and it was also true that Israel as a nation was corporately guilty of sin, and was called to repent.

From that time onwards there was a conflict between the ungodly in Israel and the righteous remnant who feared God and called on His Name. Again and again in the prophets and the psalms is heard the voice of the faithful contending bravely for God's cause and calling to Him for help in their need; and many a time we feel that we can make their words our own. In our own day we as Christians must express our humble penitence for the sins of our nation, in which we, as citizens, have been involved; and we, who believe that we are fighting a righteous conflict against a power which outrages all the laws of God, are conscious that our nation also has been deeply to blame, and shares in the common guilt. In the Old Testament, similarly, we get not only the conflict of the righteous remnant against the ungodly and their prayer to God for His cause to be vindicated and the oppressors to be punished, but also the prayer of the penitent nation accusing itself of sin: as for instance in the great liturgical prayer in Nehemiah, Chapter 9, to which reference has been made above (see page 41), and the penitential psalms, of which some at least have more than an individual reference.

It appears, then, that the Lord's enemies are not only the ungodly, but also the faithful themselves, in so far as they can truthfully accuse themselves of having taken sides against the Lord. That is not a thought which

comes easy to any of us: it is much easier to say, "we
have rebelled against the Lord", in the sense of "my
countrymen have rebelled", than to accept one's personal share of guilt, and say with Nehemiah (Chapter 1,
verse 6), "I and my father's house have sinned". Israel
was after all the Lord's people; and those who were devoted to the observance of the Law (such as the godly
Israelites of the period and the Pharisees of our Lord's
day) show a tendency which appears in some of the
psalms to contrast their own righteous ways with the
ungodliness of those who neglect the Law and of the
Gentile outsiders.

The final answer, therefore, does not come till the Old
Testament is fulfilled in the New, and the Son of God is
rejected by the outwardly religious Pharisees, but it is
not only they who are involved in guilt. The Apostles
who tell us the story of His passion confess that they all
forsook Him and fled, denied their leader publicly before
men, and one of them betrayed Him. At Calvary, therefore, all alike stand accused of sin; and He who alone
is without sin is heard praying for His murderers. The
Gospels thus imply what St. Paul makes explicit: "God
hath shut up all unto disobedience, that he might have
mercy upon all" (Roman 11:32).

Who are the Lord's enemies now? Not the poor
wretched sinners for whom He prayed, for whose salvation He died, whose sin He bore, for He counts them
not as enemies, but as His own lost sheep. The enemy is
the sin which beguiled them and led them astray; or
rather, the Enemy is the Evil One, the personal Tempter,
the "prince of this world". ,'We wrestle not against flesh
and blood"—*i.e.* human enemies—"but against princi-
palities and powers, against the world-rulers of this

darkness" (often described today as "demonic powers"),
"against the spiritual hosts of wickedness in the heavenly places" (Ephesians 6:12) ; and the Christians, fighting that battle, are bidden to take to themselves "the
whole armour of God", that is, the armour which the
Son of God wore when he came to fight His own battle
against evil (verse 13) ; for here St. Paul is quoting two
or three Old Testament texts, chiefly Isaiah 59:17, a
passage which speaks of the Lord God "putting on
righteousness as a breastplate", and coming in person to
overthrow His enemies and save His people. The second
Redemption is therefore our deliverance through the
Lord's death and resurrection, not from Egyptian enemies of Israel nor from Babylonian oppressors of
Israel, but from the Enemy of mankind himself, from
the Devil and all the hosts of evil.

Such is the final issue of the conflict against the Lord's
enemies which runs through the whole Bible ; but it is
one conflict throughout. When therefore we use the
language of this conflict, as we are bound to do, in Christian worship and prayer and thought, we are bound to
interpret the whole conflict in the light of its real meaning, as it is revealed in Jesus Christ ; and when that
is done, the phrases which describe the conflict in its
earlier stages take on a new meaning for us. We too
have our Sisera to fight : well it is for us if we imitate
Jael's zeal for her God, who is also our God. We too
have our Amalekites, and our Goliaths. The prayers in
the psalms for deliverance from enemies can all be used ;
only we must know clearly in our own minds from whom
and from what we are asking to be delivered. The prayers in the psalms for vengeance on enemies cannot be
referred to human enemies, not even to Communistic

oppressors and the like; it is necessary to see the whole problem in the light of our Lord's battle with evil, to see Him in His passion standing alone against the evil which is in men; to see how evil has led men astray, and how the Evil One has beguiled them; and then to see our own adversaries as included among those whom Satan has beguiled, and ourselves also; for we do not know their hearts, and we do know our own, and we know that we ourselves, in certain respects, have sold ourselves to sin and have thereby become tempters to others. Such a phrase in the psalms as "The kings of the earth stand up and the rulers take counsel together, against the Lord and against his Anointed" (Psalm 2:2), has got to apply also to me, in so far as I am bound in all honesty to accuse myself of having sinned and therefore of having taken sides with the Lord's enemies.

What should we do with these "cursing psalms"? We have reached this point: that these psalms belong to the literature of the conflict of the Lord against evil, and that the real meaning of the conflict is that which our Lord has revealed. Therefore they cannot be used rightly except as His psalms, since it is only He, and those who pray according to His mind, who can rightly understand who are the Lord's real enemies. The enemy, therefore, on whom our Lord in those psalms prays for vengeance is the whole power of evil. In them He pronounces judgment on that evil, He who will come again with glory to judge both the quick and the dead; and He pronounces judgment on all who persist in identifying themselves with that evil. Every one who is a sinner must therefore join in those psalms with fear of the judgment which he has deserved, and with prayer for deliverance from evil. This, then, is the traditional way of interpreting the psalms: as the prayer of Christ, and our prayer as we are united with Him as members of His body. Thus, for instance, in Fr. Benson's *War Songs of the Prince of Peace* those psalms are given headings such as "The judicial character of the Passion" or "The Wrath of the Lamb".

It needs to be added that if in some of the psalms there seems to be a note of self-complacency, as if the psalmist were quite sure that he was on the Lord's side, such self-complacency is a much more serious danger to us ordinary Christians than is vindictiveness. Neither the self-righteous Pharisee, nor we ourselves, have any right to appropriate to ourselves the words of the psalm, "Who shall ascend into the hill of the Lord? . . . Even he that hath clean hands and a pure heart" (Psalm 24:3-4). It is appointed for use on Ascension Day, manifestly in order that the words may be applied to Christ; and it would seem likely that St. John understood it in the same way, since the word for "ascend" used in the Greek version of the psalm is the same that he uses in John 20:17 and elsewhere of the Lord's ascension.

Perhaps the moral of all that we have had to say about the imperfection of the Old Testament is this: that to look out for the imperfections of the Old Testament writers is the surest of all ways to misunderstand the Old Testament. The Bible is the book of God's truth; it is the truth which the writers teach that we must look for, that truth which finds its completion and its full meaning in Christ. We have His own word for it that the Old Testament is fulfilled in Him and not destroyed. Indeed, the truths which are taught in the Old Testament are precisely the truths which our materialistic and machine-ridden modern world most needs to learn all over again: the truth of the revelation of the personal and transcendent God to Israel His people.

The synagogue came into existence in order to train up the Jewish people in the knowledge of the truths taught in the Bible; in Church services the same work is carried on. In the psalms we learn to worship God and give thanks to Him for His great glory, to meditate on His dealings with us, to confess our sin, to seek His help in our need. We are not Jews, however, but members of the re-constituted Israel of Jesus the Messiah, and all our life and our prayer is renewed and transformed by being offered to God "through Jesus Christ our Lord": that is to say, we come to God as members of Christ's body, joining in the one prayer which He makes, as the Head of the body and high priest for man. The psalter therefore becomes for us part of the prayer of Christ, the prayer which He prays and in which His Church joins. That is the practical corollary of the truth that the Old Testament is fulfilled in Christ. We shall return to the point in the next chapter (page 83).

CHAPTER VII

The Bible in the Liturgy

THE second Preface to the Book of Common Prayer (according to the use of the Church of England) thus sums up the place of the Bible in the liturgy: "The ancient fathers . . . so ordered the matter, that the whole Bible (or the greatest part thereof) should be read over once every year, intending thereby, that the Clergy, and especially such as were Ministers in the Congregation, should (by often reading, and meditation in God's word) be stirred up to godliness themselves, and be more able to exhort others by wholesome doctrine, and to confute them that were adversaries to the truth; and further, that the people (by daily hearing of holy Scripture read in the Church) might continually profit more and more in the knowledge of God, and be the more inflamed with the love of his true religion."

The liturgy is able to educate us in the knowledge of divine things, because it does not chiefly aim at instructing our minds by accurate doctrinal statements, but gives us in the first place a concrete and pictorial presentation of the Faith, which can stir our imagination and move our will. That, however, is precisely what is already done in the Bible; and the liturgy does little more than select and arrange the Biblical material. It was the Greek mind that first set itself, in the period of the Fathers, to formulate the Faith in a rationalized form, and drew up the essential definitions by which orthodox belief is guarded against heresy. Those definitions are indispensable, because heresy is that which makes the Gospel of salvation cease to be a gospel; but for our meditation and our worship we need the concrete imagery of the Bible.

Once on the Sunday after Christmas the writer of this book listened to a sermon in which the congregation was instructed in the doctrine of the Incarnation on the lines of the regular Greek theology: our Lord is the second Person of the Holy Trinity, and He has two natures in one substance. It was all very correct, but not very moving. On the same Sunday in another year he heard a sermon on the psalm-words from the introit for the day, "The Lord is King, and hath put on glorious apparel; the Lord hath put on his apparel, and girded himself with strength." The psalm, according to the meaning of the original writer, referred to God's future Coming to save His people; but we are able to understand it in the light of its fulfilment, in our Lord's birth at Bethlehem. The Son of God in becoming man, clothed Himself not with the glorious apparel of a heavenly being, but with the lowly apparel of our human nature; He girded Himself not with strength but with human weakness, that through physical weakness, spiritual strength might be made perfect. The same psalm underlies a Sarum office-hymn:

> O equal to thy Father, thou,
> Gird on thy fleshy mantle now;
> The weakness of our mortal state
> With deathless might invigorate.
>
> (St. Ambrose—Fourth century;
> translated by J. M. Neale)

Such word-pictures are necessary in the Christian liturgy, because the historical facts which we commemorate are not being thought of as mere events of history, but as present realities. Jesus Christ is the same yesterday, today and forever. On Christmas Day we are not merely keeping an anniversary of our Lord's birth; we ourselves go to Bethlehem to worship our new-born King, because His coming to be our Saviour is a present fact. In one of the hymns we pray that He may "be born in us today". So in Lent we go to the mount of the Temptation to be with Him who was tempted for us that we through His temptation might overcome the world. At Good Friday we go to Calvary; at Easter we are at the tomb and in the Upper Room; and when at Pentecost we celebrate the descent of the Holy Ghost, it is because the same Holy Ghost fills the created world and is shed abroad in our hearts today. Thus in Christian worship the past becomes present; and the future too becomes present when we adore the sacramental presence of Him who will come to be our judge and to enter on His glorious Kingdom.

Therefore the Gospel at the Eucharist comes to us as addressed directly to ourselves. On Quinquagesima Sunday, I am the blind man who hears Jesus of Nazareth passing by with His saints, on His way to Jerusalem to enter on His glory through suffering; I, because of the dullness of my blinded sight, do not grasp the situation; but I know that I am blind, and need to see, and I come with the prayer that I may receive my sight. When that has happened, it is for me to follow with His faithful people along the road to Jerusalem, in the Lent and Passiontide and Easter that are coming. Many of the Gospels tell of similar works of healing; and they all speak to us in His Sacrament, while we on our part come to Him "as sick, to the Physician of life, as blind to the Light of eternal splendor." A Gospel which contains only teaching is addressed to us as to its first hearers: 'Why beholdest

thou the mote that is in thy brother's eye, but perceivest
not the beam that is in thine own eye?" When we go to
the sacrament of Penance, we listen very attentively to
the words of advice and of warning which our father
confessor addresses to us. We need to listen even more
attentively to the words of our Lord and Master Himself.

It was a serious loss when at the Reformation the
Church of England lost the old Introits, Graduals and
other propers; for they were all scriptural, and were in
fact the remains of the psalmody of the primitive church.
Thus, to take some instances at random, the introit for
an apostle in Eastertide was: "Thou hast hidden me,
O God, from the gathering together of the froward,
alleluya; from the insurrection of the workers of iniq-
uity, alleluya, alleluya. Hear my voice, O God, in my
prayer: preserve my life from fear of the enemy. Glory
be to the Father, etc. Thou hast hidden me, etc." On the
Fifth Sunday after Easter there was sung after the
Epistle: "Alleluya, alleluya. Hitherto have ye asked
nothing in my Name: ask, and ye shall receive. Alleluya.
Christ being raised from the dead dieth no more: death
hath no more dominion over him. Alleluya" On Palm
Sunday, the anthem at the communion was: "O my
Father, if this cup may not pass away from me except I
drink it, thy will be done"; and on the Second Sunday
after Easter: "I am the Good Shepherd, alleluya; and
know my sheep, and am known of mine, alleluya".

In the same sort of way, the lessons at Morning and
Evening Prayer need to be taken up into our lives; and
there too our Prayer Book, in its zeal for simplicity, was
too ruthless in throwing away valuable things from the
old Breviary office. There, as in our lectionary, were
lessons from the Book of Lamentations in Holy Week;

but each lesson ended with the words, "O Jerusalem, Jerusalem, return unto the Lord thy God." Those few words gave just what was needed to bring the lesson out of the past into the present. The same purpose was fulfilled in the regular daily lessons in the Breviary by the responds which picked up the point of the lesson and applied it. When the early stories of David were read on the Fourth Sunday after Pentecost and the following days (in the Lectionary of the American Prayer Book, they come during the ninth and tenth weeks after Trinity Sunday), they were followed by these responds among others: "The Lord heareth all men; he sent his angel and took me from my father's sheep, and anointed me with the oil of his mercy: the Lord who delivered me from the mouth of the lion, and saved me from the paw of the bear: and anointed me with the oil of his mercy." "I took thee from thy father's house, saith the Lord, and appointed thee to be shepherd of my people: and I was with thee in all thy ways whithersoever thou wentest, establishing thy kingdom for ever. And I made thy name great, as one of the great ones of the earth: and I gave thee rest from all thy enemies. And I was with thee, etc. Glory be to the Father, etc. And I was with thee, etc." Yes, the David of whom we read was *our* David.

The Office Hymns (those appointed to a specific service—*e.g.* Mattins or Lauds—in the choir-services of the ancient Church) are not scripture, but they are nearly all scriptural; they are always free from false sentimentality, and some of them develop in a very remarkable way the "spiritual interpretation" of the Old Testament which we have seen to be characteristic of the New Testament. An Eastertide hymn begins by relating the Easter communion to the messianic wedding-feast of which our

F

Lord speaks in His parable, which we attend as did those
in the early Church who at their baptism on Easter Eve
put on a clean white robe.

> The Lamb's high banquet we await
> In snow-white robes of royal state:
> And now, the Red Sea's channel past,
> To Christ our Prince we sing at last.

We too have had our Exodus, our crossing of the Red
Sea, our Passover sacrifice:

> That Pascal eve God's arm was bared;
> The devastating Angel spared:
> By strength of hand *our* hosts went free
> From Pharaoh's ruthless tyranny.

The next verse simply paraphrases St. Paul's "Christ
our Passover is sacrificed for us"

> Now Christ our Pascal Lamb is slain,
> The Lamb of God that knows no stain;
> The true oblation offered here,
> Our own unleavened Bread sincere.

> (Seventh century—translated by J. M. Neale)

Thus it is that the Bible in the liturgy gives the Church
the language in which it expresses its thanksgiving, its
faith, its hope, its love, its meditation on the mystery of
its redemption.

Once again, with regard to intercessory prayer, it is a
mistake to think of a formula of prayer recited by the
officiating priest or of a litany, in which the people have
only the responses to make, as the ideal or indeed the
normal form of the Church's intercession. The true intercessory prayer is Morning and Evening Prayer, the daily
Office itself, and particularly the psalms in it: not, of
course, the Office as contrasted to the Eucharist, but
the Office as the further development of that central

meaning which is given in the Eucharist. Let us see
what that means.

We said in the last chapter that the psalms are to be
used as Christ's psalms (pages 74-75), since Christian
prayer is offered "through Jesus Christ our Lord", as
the prayer of the members of His body. That means
that when Christians come together to worship God, they
are not a mere collection of individuals who happen to
be worshipping together in one place; rather, they are
the Church of God, met in that place, to join in the prayer of Christ its Head. At the Eucharist, He is the in-
visible Celebrant; at the Office, the psalms are His
psalms, and the members can make those psalms and the
other prayers their own, only as they are members of
Christ. Therefore each Christian who joins in the psalms
or the *Magnificat* will be aware of his brethren in Christ
as those who share in reciting them with him; those acts
of praise and prayer are as much theirs as his, and when
he recites them, he will be thinking of their needs, and
thanking God for His goodness to them, no less than to
himself. It would be intolerable for anyone to recite
Psalm 119, all through its 176 verses, and think only of
himself; for that is the psalm which has from ancient
times been said daily in the lesser Hours from Prime to
None; and indeed its regular and rhythmical movement
can be thought of as the beating of the pulse of the
Church, Christ's body. Psalm 91, "Whoso dwelleth under the defence of the Most High", can be used on behalf
of another to beg for him the grace of God, and protection against all spiritual dangers, and (in the words of
the last three verses) that he may attain at last to Christ's
eternal kingdom.

So far we have been thinking of the regular liturgical

services, with their prescribed order, but the same principles can be applied, in some measure at least, to informal services and acts of devotion. We have been thinking of intercession, and a reform of our methods of intercession is badly needed; nothing can be worse than the common practice, in which the priest recites a form of words in which God is told what He is to be pleased to do, and the people can only answer *Amen*. Biddings, a period of silence (not three seconds or so, but half a minute, a minute, or more) in which there is time for the people to pray, and then a collect summing up the prayer, make a much better form; and a suitable psalm can often be added, with great profit.

When informal services are held, as in the meetings of "prayer groups", what is needed is that the whole action, Bible reading, remarks, prayer and praise, should form one whole; and if the Bible is to be read, it ought to take the place of honor, and any remarks be used to lead up to it and introduce it. What we have in mind can best be shown by means of a concrete instance, of an informal service used in Holy Week.

The subject is to be "The Kingdom of Christ". We begin then with a hymn such as "Rejoice, the Lord is King" (Hymn 350). A brief address follows at once, and expounds the manner of Christ's Kingdom, and how it differs from temporal power, and what sort of allegiance it demands (cf. pages 45-48 above). The address is followed immediately by the reading of the Scripture to which it is intended to lead up: John 18:29-37. Then all stand to recite Psalm 145, "I will magnify thee, O God my King', down to verse 13, with the Gloria Patri. The recitation is best if it is antiphonal, the two sides of the church alternating, and not a duet between priest and people. Then another lesson: John 19:12-20 (the Jews disown Jesus as their King, because, in the last resort, they think of Caesar as their totalitarian ruler; hence nothing remains but that Jesus should be crucified; but He is crucified with the title of King over His head, in the three languages which mattered in the ancient world) and then Psalm 72, "Give the King thy judgments, O God". At this point, it is necessary that there should be a period of silence of three to five minutes, for personal appropriation of these thoughts. Then the latter part of the *Te Deum* may be said together, from "Thou art the King of glory, O Christ", and a hymn to finish such as "The Church of God a kingdom is" (Hymn 387).

A similar scheme was used in a certain parish one winter at gatherings in houses on Sunday evenings at six-thirty. Each of the groups met under a responsible layman or laywoman, and most of the evening was usually spent in discussion; but they insisted on being provided by their priests with a liturgical introduction. The recipe for preparing a form of study was this: to take the Epistle for the Sunday, to think of two other Bible passages dealing with the same theme or otherwise relevant, and two suitable psalms; to preface one or both of the Scripture passages with a brief introduction; to add some prayers at the end, and to supply a hymn to begin and one to end. The meeting then lasted some fifteen or twenty minutes, and proved successful. One of the papers reads thusly:

Sexagesima: "Toil and danger must not frighten the ministers of God".

Hymn 563 ("He who would valiant be").

"In the Epistle today St. Paul, whose authority at

Corinth has been challenged by some rather boastful and self-important people there, tells them half-mockingly what *he* as an Apostle has got to boast (glory) about: not his cleverness or wisdom or success, but the way in which the power of God has been shown by means of his suffering and weakness."

Read 2 Corinthians 11:22-33. Recite Psalm 54.

"He continues: He may not boast even of the wonderful spiritual experience which he had had when he was caught up to the third heaven. What God had to teach him was a lesson to be learned through a tiresome and troublesome bodily ailment, which he calls a "thorn in the flesh".

Read 2 Corinthians 12:1-11. Recite Psalm 30. Pray for those who are critical of the Church and its mission in the world. Pray for humility—that poverty of spirit which is a mark of blessedness. Pray for the lapsed. Collects for Septuagesima and Epiphany VI. Hymn 164 ("To thee before the close of day").

The subjects for the four Sundays in Advent were:
Advent I. "The Lord's Coming to His Church."

Hymn 9. Luke 12:35-48. Psalm 2. Luke 13:23-28.
Psalm 97. Hymn 7.

Advent II. "Comfort through Scriptures."

Hymn 301. Luke 11:14-28. Psalm 46. 2 Timothy 3:10-17. Psalm 119:105-112. Hymn 399.

Advent III. "Call to Service."

Hymn 10. Isaiah 35:3-10. Psalm 80. Matthew 10:1-17. Hymn 201.

Advent IV. "The Lord is at hand."

Hymn 10. Isaiah 33:13-17. Psalm 96. Revelation 21:6-end. Psalm 43. Hymn 1.

CHAPTER VIII

The Bible in the Church Today

WE have seen in the course of our study how the Bible has been from the very beginning the Book of the Faith, for the instruction of the people of the Israel of God in the truth about Him and His redemptive work and the way of His spiritual service; how it was for that purpose that the books were originally brought together into a Canon of Scripture; how the Jewish synagogue existed in order to bring the Bible to the people; how the Church carried on the synagogue tradition, using the Old Testament books and adding to them the books of the Apostles; how the Breviary thus grew up, to carry on the tradition of the use of the Old Testament which is given in the New; and how it was the purpose of the Anglican reformers to carry on the "godly and decent order of the ancient Fathers", and to restore it where it had been partially lost; for they point out how it had been overlaid with legendary matter and the lessons cut down, so that "commonly when any book of the Bible was begun, after three or four chapters were read out, the rest was unread" (from the second Preface to the English Prayer Book).

In their zeal to achieve that end they carried out an over-drastic pruning, abolishing the office hymns, antiphons and responds from the office, and all the psalmody from the Holy Communion. Nevertheless, Morning and Evening Prayer have been for nearly 400 years the glory of the Anglican Communion, and have provided for clergy and people the nourishment of psalms and scriptures. The value of their use is strikingly seen when we compare the text of Handel's *Messiah* with that of Bach's

Passion according to St. Matthew. The words to which Bach's wonderful arias and chorales are set are pietistic, sentimental, and utterly unworthy of the Gospel text which is sung in the recitative; the reason for that is simply that the Lutheran churches had lost the breviary office at the Reformation, and had thus almost completely dropped the Old Testament out of their service; but Handel's *Messiah* is based on the Anglican tradition, and his music is set to the splendid texts of the Old Testament prophecies.

Be that as it may, the good tradition which we have inherited is being corrupted and is in danger of being lost; and it is our own generation that is to blame for the evil work. Until the period after the First World War, the psalms for the day were regularly used, and no one thought of shortening them; and there was a regular course of Sunday lessons which became very familiar, since almost no alternatives were provided. Nowadays, a special psalm (or two) is appointed for every day, so that even in those churches where the daily Offices are read, the psalter is becoming largely lost to the people.

As for the lessons, the provision of alternatives means that the lessons are not known as they used to be; yet the old tradition, dating from the synagogue, was that the Scriptures should become so familiar as to be known almost by heart. Many priests choose between the alternative lessons simply as seems good to them, or else choose lessons of their own devising, which is disastrous.

The corruption of our liturgical tradition in such respects could never have come about, had it not been for the paralysing uncertainty about the Bible, and particularly about the Old Testament, which exists in the minds of the clergy and laity, and of which something was said in our first chapter. It is possibly the most urgent of all needs in the Church of today that the rot should be stopped, and the damage which has been done repaired. The failure to make the right use of the Scriptures in the liturgy bars the way to the right understanding of them; but also, the right understanding of them will quickly make the present misuse of them intolerable.

There is hope for the future, in the fact that there is an increasing realization of the seriousness of the problem. There is a general awareness among Biblical scholars of the need for a better theological understanding of the Bible. It is being realized to how great an extent the standard books on the Bible have not dealt with the study of the Bible itself, but with various preliminaries to the study of it, such as the sorting out of the various writers whose work has been put together in the editing of the books, or the collection from primitive religion of parallels to Jacob's pouring of oil on a sacred stone at Bethel. The gathering of information about such things should be expected to throw light in many ways on the meaning of the text itself; and so it does. So many books about the Bible have been filled with that sort of information, however, that it has come to be thought that those things are in themselves the study of the Bible; and it has even happened that school text-books have been filled with that sort of information about sources and documents and fetishes and totems, and have contained next to nothing of the real knowledge of the Bible. Consequently one of the more terrible of the sayings of Amos has come to pass among us: "Behold, the days come, saith the Lord, that I will send a famine in the land: not a famine of bread, nor a thirst for water, but of hearing the words of the Lord" (Amos 8:11). We suffer now from that spiritual famine; for the real knowledge of the Bible is that which springs from reading it, studying it, and using it as the Book of the Israel of God, the Book of the Faith.

Happily, things are changing. Every year sees an improvement of the situation in the learned world, in the shape of some book in which the Bible is studied from the point of view of Israel's Faith. Some excellent popular books have recently appeared, and we can hope soon to see a new type of textbook for use in schools.

The right use of the Bible, however, does not lie only in the right study of it in universities, in schools, and in parochial and other study circles, important though that is; nor does it lie only in the use of it for devotional reading and meditation, though in one form or another they are an indispensable part of the prayer-life of every Christian; for every Christian needs to know for himself what his faith is, and in what particular ways his faith and his religion are to bear their fruit in the consecration of all his life and all his work to the glory of God. The use of the Bible which gives the key to that and to all the rest, is its use in the Church's services, for the molding of the common life of the believing and worshipping community in each place by that which it does and says and hears in church. It seems that in the immediate future we are to see a strong development of the consciousness of Christians that to belong to the Church means to share in a common life of faith, whereby they are united with one another as members of a body through whose veins one life-blood flows. That common life is nourished by the Word and the Sacraments: by the Word of God which speaks through the Scriptures, and at the altar by the Bread of Life and the Cup of Salvation.

An encouraging sign of the times is the appearance of "parish meetings" which are coming into existence for the realization of "the true nature of the Church as the body of Christ", by getting the people to meet together regularly in order to know one another as Christians. It is an astonishing fact that we should talk as we do of the Church as God's family, and as Christ's body, and yet scarcely know the Christians with whom we regularly worship; or if we do, to chat with them about the weather, or football, but never to go deeper and speak of the things that matter, and of the meaning of our Faith and its relevance to daily difficulties. It is astonishing that so much labor should be given to the production of sermons, and yet that the sermons which are preached should not be discussed. People will tell the preacher that they liked his sermon, and not tell him what it was that they liked in it, or if there were some things in it with which they disagreed, or which they did not understand.

It is this whole way of going on that is challenged by the parish meeting. It is simply the coming-together of those who meet in fellowship at the altar, to get to know one another as Christians, and get back to the spiritual root of the Church's existence by learning the meaning of that fellowship which is established at the altar. In a growing number of places the secret is being sought and discovered; a parish meeting comes together in which all sorts of things (in the parish church and out of it, in the parish, in the town, in the nation) are discussed, and the endeavor made to see them from a Christian point of view.

What is, then, the Christian point of view from which they are to be seen? What is it that distinguishes parish

meetings from mere debating societies where persons
who hold views are able to air them? It is that their
object is to find out the Church's mind, the Christian way
of looking at things, the "mind of Christ"; and the rec-
ollection that the starting-point of the whole quest is
the fellowship which the Lord creates, in the Sacrament
of the Altar, is seen to demand that the meeting should do
other things than discuss problems. It must also pray
about them; and the members in many places take turns
to pray, in their own words. It must also learn to know
the Bible; and one meeting after another finds it necessary to return to the Scripture and to take it up seriously.

This book will have been written in vain if it does not
now appear that the study of the Word of God in the
Old Testament and the New, is, with the Sacrament, the
greatest need of all. If the parish meeting is seeking the
spiritual root of the Church's existence it must learn from
the Bible what the Church is. The Church is the continuation of the Old Israel in which the Old Testament books
were written. The Israel of God has thirty-four centuries
of continuous existence behind it. It looks back to its
beginning in its Redemption out of Egypt. It reckons
among its heroes Moses, Samuel, David, Elijah, Isaiah.
It has heard the prophets announce the future coming of
the Saviour. It has seen the Saviour come; it goes to
meet Him in His present coming at the altar, when the
mystery of Christmas, and of Calvary, and of Easter,
and of Pentecost, is renewed here and now in the Christian assembly. It acknowledges as its spiritual head in
each place a successor of the Apostles whom Jesus sent
into the world. It believes itself to be the local unit of
that messianic community, that renewed Israel, which
the prophets announced beforehand and Jesus the Mes-

siah inaugurated. It proclaims that He reigns as the true
King over all the world.

As we are "fellow-citizens with the saints, and of the
household of God", so the Bible is our book. We begin
to enter into its meaning only when we see it from within. The psalmist is one of us; he fought in his day the
same battle of the Lord which we have to fight in ours,
and we take to ourselves his thoughts, and use his words.
The biblical historian is one of us; he did not write from
the point of view of the secular historian, but judged
the course of events which he recorded from that point of
view which we ourselves regard as that which is finally
important, namely, seeking to see what God was doing
in the events: how God was judging men for their sins,
and saving them in the midst of His judgments. The
Bible is the book of the Israel of God; the Church is the
Israel of God; and so the Bible is the Church's book.

In an earlier chapter, reference was made to Psalm
102 (see page 38 above). That psalm was written in
exile; and as we too (according to a legitimate "spiritual"
interpretation) are in exile in Babylon, we can rightly
use its words of our own condition. "My heart is smitten
down," cries the Church of today, "and withered like
grass, so that I forget to eat my bread"; my children
have forgotten how to read their Bible, and "break the
bread of the word"; they are suffering from a famine
of the word of God. But "thou, O Lord, shall endure for
ever: and thy remembrance unto all generations"; and
Thy saving purpose will go on: "Thou shalt arise, and
have mercy upon Zion", on Israel Thy people, on Thy
Church. The time is coming when "the Lord shall build
up Zion, and when his glory shall appear"; great times
are coming for the Church of God, when "the people

which shall be born shall praise the Lord", and the nations gather "to declare the Name of the Lord in Zion,
and his worship at Jerusalem"—that is, at the altar,
where the Sacrifice of the Messiah is celebrated, and
shall be celebrated by the generations yet to come. The
sign of it all is that to which our Lord pointed in His
parable of the mustard seed, when He compared the outwardly insignificant preaching of the Kingdom of God
in Galilee with the immense future growth of the Kingdom of the Christ on earth in the centuries to come and
in the glory of eternity. The seed holds the promise of
the future; and the seed is there, growing. So it is with
the Church today; there is wreckage all around, but we
know that there is no other Gospel, no other answer to
the problem of our dark and sinful world, but this. Christ
is the answer, and He has the words of eternal life. So,
returning to the psalm, the fact that "thy servants think
upon her stones, and it pitieth them to see her in the
dust"—the fact that Christians everywhere are grieved
about the Church's sad condition, and are seeking to return to the Bible and to see it as the Book of the Faith—
means that those thoughts in the minds of God's children
would not be there unless God had put them there. God's
purpose will go on: "the children of thy servants shall
continue: and their seed shall stand fast in thy sight."